Chronology of Scottish History

DAVID ROSS

GEDDES & GROSSET

Published 2002 by Geddes & Grosset

ISBN 1 85534 380 0

Printed in Poland, OZGraf S.A.

Contents

Chronology of Scottish History

AD 79
Julius Agricola begins the Roman conquest of North Britain.

84
Battle of Mons Graupius. Romans defeat Caledonians.

c.85
Agricola builds a line of forts between the Forth and the Clyde.

105
Romans forced out of southern Scotland.

122
Commencement of building of Hadrian's Wall.

c.126
Disappearance of the Ninth Legion.

127
Completion of Hadrian's Wall.

139
Lollius Urbicus moves north with three legions: Antonine Wall begun.

c.143
Completion of Antonine Wall.

c.150
Ptolemy of Alexandria records place and tribal names in his *Universal Geography*.

c.155
Tribal uprisings force Roman retreat from southern Scotland.

158
Romans return and re-garrison Antonine Wall.

180
Romans forced back behind Hadrian's Wall.

196
Maeatae overrun Hadrian's Wall.

208
Emperor Septimius Severus rebuilds Hadrian's Wall and invades Caledonia.

210
Caracalla, future emperor, tries to exterminate the Maeatae and Caledonii.

c.258
Possible first colonisation by Scots, under Reuda.

296
Further rebuilding of Hadrian's Wall.

305–06
Constantius Chlorus campaigns against Picts.

c.350
Birth of St Ninian.

360
Picts and Scots invade across Hadrian's Wall, reaching as far as London.

364–67
Picts and Scots make further raids.
The tribes of the Verturiones and the Attacotti are first mentioned.

369
Theodosius reinstates the frontier.

378
St Ninian goes to Rome.

382
Magnus Maximus drives back the Picts and the Scots.

383
Hadrian's Wall again broken through, no longer reconstructed.
Frontier troops withdrawn.

397
St Ninian's Church at Whithorn dedicated to St Martin.

407
Roman legions withdraw from the island of Britain.

410
End of Roman rule in Britain.

c.420
Irish king, Niall of the Nine Hostages, raids in the west.

431
Death of St Ninian at Whithorn.

432
St Patrick sails to Ireland.

498
The Scots settlement begins. Formation of kingdom of Dàl
Riada.

c.521
Birth of St Columba in Ireland

547
The Angles control Lothian.

c.550
Hostile relations between Picts and Scots.

561
St Moluag founds a monastery on Lismore.

563

St Columba comes to Iona and founds a monastery.

565

St Columba's mission to the Pictish king.

573

Rhydderch, King of Strathclyde, recorded as winning a battle at Arderydd, perhaps Arthuret, Cumbria

574

Death of Conall, King of Scots. Accession of King Aedan.

575

'Synod' of Drumceatt: Scots of Dàl Riada cease to pay tribute to High King of Ulster.

c.580

Aedan, King of Scots, recorded as fighting in Orkney.

584

Death of Bridei, King of Picts, at Battle of Asreth in Circinn (Angus). Accession of Gartnait.

597

Death of St Columba.

c.600

Defeat of the Gododdin tribe by Northumbrians.

c.602

Foundation of a church at Dunblane by St Blane.

603

Defeat of Aedan by the Angles at Degsastam.

608

Death of St Baldred.

612

Death of St Kentigern.

c.613

Welsh-speaking Cumbria and Cambria cut off from each other by Northumbrian expansion.

c.617

Eanfrith flees from Northumbria to Pictland.
Monks on Eigg massacred, probably by pagan Picts.

623

Death of Fergna, first recorded Bishop of Iona.

634

St Aidan sent from Iona to convert the Northumbrians.

640

Battle in Glen Moriston between Picts and Scots.

657

Oswiu, King of Northumberland, becomes Overlord of the Scots.

664

Synod of Whitby establishes the Roman practice in place of that of the Celtic Church.

671

Egcfrith of Northumbria conquers the southern Picts.

672

Deposition of Drest, King of Picts. Accession of Bridei MacBili.

673

Foundation of monastery at Applecross by St Maelrubha.

681

Trumwine is the first bishop of the Northumbrian 'Pictish Province'.

682

Bridei MacBili campaigns in Orkney.

684

Battle of Nechtansmere: the Picts defeat the Northumbrians.
Death of Tuathal, first recorded Bishop of Fothrif (and Abbot of Dunkeld).

697

Completion of Adamnan's *Life of Saint Columba*.

c.700

The Brecbennach or Monymusk Reliquary is made.
Curitain is first recorded Bishop of Ross.

710

King Nechton of the Picts expels the Ionan clergy and makes the Pictish Church conform to Roman practice.

711

Scots defeat Britons at Loch Arklet.

721

A Pictish bishop attends a gathering in Rome.

728

Civil war among the Picts as Alpin, Drust and Oengus contend for the kingship.

731

King Oengus takes the Pictish throne and overlordship of the Scots.
The Venerable Bede's *History of the English Church* provides valuable information on Scotland.

735

Reputed date of a battle between the Picts and Northumbrians, still commemorated at Athelstaneford.

736

Oengus ravages Dàl Riada, capturing Dunadd.

739

Earliest mention of Fotla (Atholl), whose king, Talorcan, is drowned at the order of Oengus, King of Picts.

741
Oengus defeats the Scots.

748
Aed Finn MacEochaid becomes King of the Scots

756
With the help of the Northumbrians, King Oengus subdues the Britons of Strathclyde.

*c.***760**
Founding of the cult of St Andrew at Kilrymont (St Andrews).

776
Battles between Picts and Scots.

781
Death of Fergus, King of Scots. Scots under Pictish rule.

794
Viking attacks begin.

795
Iona attacked by Vikings.

*c.***800**
Compilation of the *Book of Kells* on Iona.

806
Monastery of Iona sacked by Norsemen.

818
Abbot Diarmit leaves Iona for the mainland.

839
Picts defeated by Norsemen.
Kenneth MacAlpin becomes King of Scots.

*c.***843**
Kenneth MacAlpin becomes King of Picts and Scots.

846

Founding of Dunkeld Cathedral.

c.860

Death of Kenneth MacAlpin. Accession of Donald I; new law of succession.

862

Death of Donald I. Accession of Constantine I.

865

First specific mention of Dunkeld as a religious centre and of the Bishop/Abbot of Fortriu.

866

Ketill Flatnose ravages Pictish territory.

c.875

Orkney becomes a Norse Earldom.

877

Constantine I dies fighting Norsemen. Accession of Aed.

878

Death of Aed. Accession of Giric.

889

Accession of Donald II.

c.890

Orkney, Shetland, Hebrides and Caithness become part of Harold Fairhair's kingdom of Norway.

900

Donald II dies fighting Norsemen. Accession of Constantine II.

903

Norsemen sack Dunkeld.
Around this time, St Andrews becomes the religious capital.

918

Scots and Britons defeat Vikings at Corbridge.

926
Athelstan takes possession of Northumbria.

934
Athelstan invades from Northumbria.

937
Battle of Brunanburh: Northumbrians defeat Scots and Britons.
Abdication of Constantine II. Accession of Malcolm I.

945
Cumberland is ceded to Malcolm I.

954
Death of Malcolm I. Accession of Indulf.

*c.***963**
Death of Indulf. Accession of Dubh.

967
Death of Dubh. Accession of Culein.

971
Death of Culein. Accession of Kenneth II.

*c.***971**
Edgar cedes Lothian to Kenneth II.

987
Earl Sigurd of Orkney controls Sutherland, Ross and parts of
  Moray.

995
Death of Kenneth II. Accession of Constantine III 'the Bald'.

997
Death of Constantine III.
Short reigns of Kenneth III and Grig follow.

1000
Around this time, a two-hundred-year spell of warmer
  weather begins over western and northern Europe.

1005

Death of Grig. Accession of Malcolm II.

1006

Malcolm II invades Bernicia. He is defeated at Durham.

1014

Battle of Clontarf in Ireland ends Norse overlordship there.
Malcolm II campaigns in the Western Isles.

1018

Battle of Carham.
Lothian permanently incorporated into Scots kingdom.

1028

Maelduin is first recorded Bishop of St Andrews.

1033

Invasion of Cnut, King of Denmark and England. Malcolm II
pays homage.

1034

Death of Malcolm II. Accession of Duncan I, first king to rule
over both Alba and Strathclyde.
The name Scotland comes into use around now.

1040

Death of Duncan I. Accession of Macbeth.

1045

Battle of Dunkeld between pro- and anti-Macbeth armies.

1054

Earl Siward of Northumbria invades on Malcolm Canmore's
behalf. Lothian and Strathclyde are taken over.

1057

Death of Macbeth in a battle at Lumphanan. Brief reign of
Lulach in the north.

1058

Battle of Eassie. Death of Lulach. Accession of Malcolm III 'Canmore'.

1060

Earl Thorfinn builds a cathedral on Birsay in Orkney.

1061

Malcolm III invades Northumbria. Marries Ingibiorg of Orkney about this time.

1069

Malcolm III invades Northumbria and Cumbria.

Following Ingibiorg's death, Malcolm III marries Princess Margaret.

1070

Malcolm III invades Northumbria and Cumbria.

1073

William I invades. Malcolm III does homage at Abernethy.

1079

Malcolm III invades Northumbria.

1091

Further invasion of Northumbria by Malcolm III.

1092

William Rufus takes possession of Cumberland and builds a castle at Carlisle.

1093

Death of Malcolm III at Alnwick in Northumberland.
Accession of Donald III 'Ban'.

1094

Brief installation of Duncan II, his assassination and the resumption of rule by Donald III.

1097

Oldest extant charter of Scotland: a royal grant of land to the
monks of St Cuthbert.

1097

Deposition and blinding of Donald III. Accession of Edgar.

1098

Magnus III 'Barelegs' of Norway devastates the Western
Isles. The Isles are ceded to Magnus by Edgar.

1099

Death of Donald III: last king to be buried on Iona.

1105

Edgar sends an elephant to the High King of Ireland, as a gift.

1107

Death of Edgar. Accession of Alexander I.

1109

First recorded Bishop of Glasgow, Michael.

1113

Selkirk Abbey founded.

1114

The future David I becomes Earl of Huntingdon in England.
Culdee monastery at Scone rebuilt by Alexander I.

c.1115

Murder of Earl Magnus of Orkney by Earl Haakon.

1124

Death of Alexander I. Accession of David I.
First recorded Bishop of Moray, Gregory.
Aberdeen and Perth made royal burghs.
The office of Sheriff is first recorded around this time.

1128

Holyrood Abbey founded. Kelso Abbey founded (removed
from Selkirk).

1130

Rebellion of Angus of Moray and Malcolm MacHeth.

Founding of Bishopric of the Isles (including Isle of Man): a Norwegian diocese.

Book of Deer compiled around this time, a Gospel text with the oldest Scottish Gaelic writings in the margin.

1132

First recorded Bishop of Aberdeen, Nechtan.

1134

The Crown annexes the Earldom of Moray.

1135

David I begins to harry northern England.

1136

Melrose Abbey founded.

1138

The Battle of the Standard (August 22).

Founding of St Magnus Cathedral, Kirkwall, and Jedburgh Abbey.

1139

Henry, Prince of Scotland, becomes Earl of Northumbria.

1140

Wimund the Monk a claimant to the throne about this time.

Bishopric of Caithness established at Dornoch.

Founding of Dryburgh Abbey.

1142

Dundrennan Abbey founded by David I.

1147

Founding of Cambuskenneth Abbey.

1150

First recorded Bishop of Brechin, Samson.

1151

Founding of Kinloss Abbey (from Melrose). First recorded Bishop of Caithness, Andrew.

1153

Death of David I. Accession of Malcolm IV 'the Maiden'.

1155

First recorded Bishop of Dunblane, Laurence.

1156

Somerled establishes himself as Lord of the Isles.
Grammar school founded in Aberdeen.

1157

Release of Malcolm MacHeth from Roxburgh Castle.

1158

Walter FitzAlan is made High Steward.
Somerled invades the Isle of Man and takes control of it.

1159

Malcolm IV joins Henry II's invasion of France.
Treaty between Malcolm IV and Somerled.

1160

Revolt of six earls is put down.
Galloway revolt put down, with English assistance.
Earliest likely date of the founding of Saddell Abbey, Kintyre.

1163

Founding of Paisley Abbey by Walter FitzAlan.

1164

Revolt, defeat and death of Somerled, Lord of Argyll, whilst raiding Renfrew.

1165

Death of Malcolm IV. Accession of William I 'the Lion'.

1171
First record of Jews in Scotland. Abraham of Edinburgh lends £80 to Robert de Quincy.

1174
Capture of William I at Alnwick by the English and subsequent imprisonment. Under the terms of the Treaty of Falaise, William accepts English overlordship.

1178
Arbroath Abbey founded by William I.

1179
MacWilliam rising in the north.

William I excommunicated in dispute over Bishopric of St Andrews; Scotland under interdict.

1181
Roland of Galloway defeats Donald Ban MacWilliam; rising ends.

1187
Rebellion in Moray put down with help of Galloway men.

1189
The Quitclaim of Canterbury releases William I from his allegiance to England.

Council held at Musselburgh agrees tax to pay Scotland's 'ransom'.

1190
Berwick and Roxburgh established as royal burghs.

1191
Dundee established as a royal burgh.

1192
Scottish Church made a 'special daughter' of Rome.

First recorded Bishop of Lismore, Harald.

1196

William I takes control of the north from Harold, Earl of Orkney.

1200

First reference in charters to coal mining: as a perquisite of the monks of Holyrood.

1203

Ragnall, son of Somerled, founds a Benedictine abbey on Iona.

1211

Guthred MacWilliam, descended from Duncan II, establishes power in Ross.

1212

Defeat and death of Guthred.

1214

Death of William I. Accession of Alexander II.
Invasion of Moray by Donald MacWilliam and Kenneth MacHeth.

1215

MacWilliam and MacHeth defeated by Fearchar MacTaggart.

1216

Cistercian monastery founded at Culross.

1217

Alexander II leads a Scots army as far as Dover.

1220

Carles who fail to join the army when summoned are to be fined a cow and a sheep.

1221

Alexander II marries Joanna of England.

1222

Murder of the Bishop of Caithness; Alexander II leads a force there to assert authority.

1224

Seat of the Bishop of Moray is moved from Spynie to Elgin.
Rathven Hospital, Banff, founded for the care of lepers.

c. **1227**

Founding of Balmerino Abbey.

1230

Foundation of Beauly and Ardchattan Priories.

1233

'Master of schools' recorded at Ayr.

1234

Last Celtic Lord of Galloway dies. Revolt in Galloway
defeated.

1236

Bridge recorded at Ayr.
Bishopric of Lismore re-established.

1237

Treaty of York fixes Scottish border with England.

1238

Death of Joanna. Alexander II marries a French bride.

1242

Alexander II offers to buy the Hebrides from Norway.

1244

Peace concord with England.

1247

Record of shipbuilding at Inverness.

1249

Death of Alexander II. Accession of Alexander III.

1250

Canonisation of St Margaret.

1251

Alexander III marries Princess Margaret of England (25 December).

1255

Durward, supported by England, ousts Comyn as Alexander III's 'adviser'.

1257

Comyn regency successful over Durward.

1258

Death of Comyn. Alexander III establishes personal rule.

1263

Haakon IV reasserts control over the Western Isles. Battle of Largs.

1266

Treaty of Perth – Scotland gains the Hebrides and Isle of Man for a lump sum and an annual payment.

1274

Devorguilla Balliol founds Sweetheart Abbey.

Value of church lands put at £18,662; King's revenue £5,413.

Birth of Robert Bruce (11 July). Probable birth year of William Wallace.

1275

Benemund de Vicci sent from Rome to reassess Scottish Church income and payments to the papacy.

1278

Alexander III visits Edward I in London.

1281

Princess Margaret of Scotland marries King Eric of Norway (she dies 1283).

1286

Death of Alexander III. Accession of Margaret, daughter of Eric and Margaret, the 'Maid of Norway'.

1289

Treaty of Salisbury.

1290

Treaty of Birgham (March): Maid of Norway to marry crown prince of England.

First documentary record of a parliament.

Death in Orkney of Margaret, Maid of Norway. The kingship in dispute.

1291

Edward I of England in control of Scotland. Thirteen 'Competitors' claim the crown.

1292

Edward I of England's traversal of Scotland reaches as far as Elgin.

Kingship of Scots awarded to John Balliol; he is crowned in November.

Sheriffdoms are set up in Argyll and Skye.

1295

First recorded French-Scottish alliance.

Record of Court of Four Burghs meeting in Edinburgh.

1296

Battle of Dunbar.

Deposition of John Balliol by Edward I of England.

Removal of Scotland's regalia and records, and of the Stone of Destiny.

Compilation of the 'Ragman Roll'.

Sacking of Berwick.

1297

Risings of William Wallace and Andrew Murray. Attack on the Justiciar at Scone.

Defeat of Robert Bruce at Irvine. Victory of Stirling Bridge (11 September).

Death of Andrew Murray. Wallace named as Guardian.

1298

Edward I invades again and defeats Wallace at Falkirk (22 July). Sir John Soulis becomes Guardian.

1299

Scots take Stirling Castle.

1300

Edward I agrees a truce to 1301. Pope Boniface VIII claims right of arbitration.

1301

Sir John Soulis, Guardian, sends emissaries to Rome to plead Scotland's case before the Pope.

1302

Robert Bruce submits to Edward I.

1303

Scots victory at Battle of Roslin (24 February). Edward I embarks on subjugation of Scotland.

1304

Stirling Castle retaken by the English. Bruce and Bishop Lamberton make a band of alliance.

1305

Edward I's Ordinance for the government of Scotland.

Capture and execution (23 August) of Wallace.

1306

Robert Bruce murders John 'the Red' Comyn at Dumfries (10 February).

Robert I (Bruce) crowned at Scone (25 March).
Battle of Methven (19 June).

1307
Battle of Loudon Hill (May). Edward I of England dies (July).
Robert I campaigns in the north.
Battle of Inverurie (24 December). Robert I commands the
  'herschip' or ravaging of Buchan.

1308
Battle of the Pass of Brander (15 August).
Death of Duns Scotus.

1309
Robert I's first parliament (16–17 March).

1310
Edward II campaigns in Scotland, until 1311.

1311
Raids into England this year and next.

1312
Treaty of Inverness, with Norway (29 October).

1313
Recapture of Perth (January).

1314
Roxburgh and Edinburgh Castles retaken.
Scots' victory at Battle of Bannockburn (23–24 June).

1316
Edward Bruce crowned king of Ireland.

1318
Berwick recaptured (March).
Death of Edward Bruce.
Pope John XXII places Scotland under interdict.
First mention of Lyon King of Arms, chief herald of Scotland.

1320

Consecration of St Andrews Cathedral.

1320

Declaration of Arbroath (6 April).
Soulis Conspiracy and Black Parliament (August).

1322

Raids into England, as far as Lancaster. Invasion attempt by Edward II fails.

1323

Andrew Harcla tries to negotiate a peace for England.

1324

Bruce's kingship recognized by the Pope.

1326

Representation of burghs in parliament.
Treaty of Corbeil reaffirms French alliance.
Robert I establishes his home on the Clyde.
Around this time, Skye forms a separate bishopric within the archdiocese of Trondheim.

1327

Invasion of England. Scots troops find cannon used against them for the first time.
Dundee receives charter confirming royal burgh status.

1328

Scottish kingdom recognized by England (17 March) in the Treaty of Edinburgh–Northampton.

1329

Death of Robert I (7 June). Accession of David II, first King of Scots to be crowned with full papal sanction (24 November).
Building of Brig o' Balgownie, Aberdeen.

1332

Invasion and coronation of Edward Balliol. Renewal of war with England.

Baliol wins the Battle of Dupplin Moor (11 August).
Flight of Balliol (December).

1333

Scots defeated at Battle of Halidon Hill (19 July). English
retake Berwick.
Return of Edward Balliol.

1334

David II and Queen Joan are sent to take refuge in France
(May).
Earliest known Scots armorial bearings, on a seal of the Earl of
Mar.

1335

Invasion of Edward III reaches Perth. Sir Andrew Murray
heads resistance.
Imports of Scandinavian timber recorded.

1336

Edward III causes destruction as far north as Elgin.
First use of the title *Dominus Insularum* (Lord of the Isles) by
John of Islay.

1337

John, Lord of the Isles, negotiates with the English Earl of
Salisbury.

1338

'Black Agnes', Countess of Dunbar, defends Dunbar Castle
against the Earls of Salisbury and Arundel.
Death of Sir Andrew Murray.

1340

Existence of a hospital noted at Bara (East Lothian).

1341

Edinburgh Castle retaken (April).
Restoration of David II (June).

1346

Scots defeated at Battle of Neville's Cross (17 October). Capture of David II. Robert the Steward assumes administration.

1349

Ravages of bubonic plague reach Scotland for the first time.

1350

Revival of Lordship of the Isles.

1352

David II's temporary return (February).

1354

French alliance renewed. Negotiations for David II's return fail.

1356

Edward Balliol renounces his 'kingship'.
Edward III's punitive expedition: the 'Burnt Candlemas'.

1357

Treaty signed (October) for David II's ransom and release.
Return of David II.
First mention of a grammar school at Cupar.

1359

David II makes diplomatic visit to London (February).

1360

Murder of David II's mistress, Katherine Mortimer.
Oronsay Priory established by John of Islay, Lord of the Isles.
New bubonic plague outbreaks.

1362

First recorded feu charter: land granted in perpetuity.

1363

David II faces down the Steward and his allies; marries Margaret Logie.

1364

Parliament refuses a union with England and confirms the Steward (the future Robert II) as heir presumptive to the crown.

Last recorded lawsuit for recovery of a runaway serf.

Burgh merchants given monopoly of buying and selling within their burghs.

1365

The French chronicler Jean Froissart visits Scotland and writes his impressions.

1369

David II comes in force to Inverness. The Lord of the Isles brought to submission.

Lanark and Linlithgow replace English-held Berwick and Roxburgh in the Court of Four Burghs (other two are Edinburgh and Stirling).

1370

David II makes diplomatic visit to London.

Composition of *The Pistill of Suete Susan*, about this time, one of the earliest Scots literary texts.

1371

Death of David II (22 February). Accession of Robert II (the Steward: the first king of the Stewart dynasty).

Treaty of Vincennes (28 October) renews Franco-Scottish alliance.

1375

John Barbour's *The Brus* appears.

1378

Export of hides at 44,559, compared to 8,861 in 1327.

Donald MacDonald, son of the Lord of the Isles, is given a safe-conduct through England to attend Oxford University.

1379

Henry Sinclair of Roslin becomes Earl of Orkney, as vassal of the King of Norway.

1381

John of Gaunt takes refuge in Edinburgh from the Peasants' Revolt.

1383

Walter Wardlaw appointed first Scottish Cardinal.

1384

Parliament deplores lawlessness of the time; an Act is passed for the suppression of 'masterful plunderers or caterans'.

Franco-Scottish raids into Northern England.

John of Gaunt invades and holds Edinburgh to ransom.

1385

French force arrives in Scotland. Richard II invades, sacks Edinburgh and retreats.

Reconstruction of the church of St Giles, Edinburgh.

1387

The chronicler, John of Fordun, author of the *Scotichronicon*, dies.

1388

Robert Stewart, Earl of Fife, appointed Guardian.

Battle of Otterburn (5 August).

1390

Death of Robert II. Accession of Robert III.

Destruction of Elgin Cathedral by Alexander, the 'Wolf of Badenoch', the brother of Robert III

1391

Earl of Orkney's expedition to Greenland or North America, with the Venetian Antonio Zeno.

1396

Staged clan battle on the North Inch at Perth between Kay and Chattan clans (September).

1397

Disorders of the times deplored in general council.

1398

Stewart Earls of Carrick and Fife raised to Dukes of Rothesay and Albany.

1399

Duke of Rothesay becomes King's Lieutenant.

1400

Henry IV of England invades and retreats (August).

1401

Albany Herald mentioned for the first time, among Scots heralds.

1402

Duke of Rothesay dies in custody at Falkland (March).
Scots defeated at Battle of Homildon Hill (14 September).

1404

Duke of Albany becomes the King's Lieutenant.

1405

Royal burghs south of the Spey are required to send a delegate to the Court of the Four Burghs.

1406

Capture at sea of Prince James (14 March).
Death of Robert III (4 April). Accession of James I (imprisoned in England). Albany appointed Governor by Parliament.
James Resby, English Lollard priest, burnt to death at Perth (possibly 1407).

1408

Only surviving record of a Gaelic charter from the Lord of the Isles.

1409

Earl of Mar (later Admiral of Scotland) captures a ship owned by London's Lord Mayor Whittington.

1410

Disputes with Dutch over the North Sea fishing grounds.

1412

Because of constant Scottish piracy, the Hanseatic Diet seeks to suspend trade with Scotland.

1411

Battle of Harlaw (24 July) between forces led by the Lord of the Isles and the Earl of Mar.

Scotland's first university founded, at St Andrews, by Bishop Wardlaw.

1413

Papal bull confirms St Andrews University.

1415

Hanseatic trade forbidden to Scots because of piracy, until 1436.

1417

Border raids and disorder until 1422.

1418

End of the Great Schism: Scotland is last country to accept authority of Pope Martin V.

Earl of Buchan leads a Scots army to France.

1420

Death of Duke of Albany (September). Murdoch Stewart becomes Duke of Albany and Governor.

Robert Henryson born (dies c.1490).

1421

Scots army in France defeats English at Baugé (22 March).

1422

Scots first recorded as forming French king's bodyguard.

At this time, Andrew of Wyntoun (*c.*1350–*c.*1424) compiles his *Orygenale Cronykil of Scotland*.

c.1423

Composition of *The Kingis Quair* by James I.

1424

James I returns from captivity (April). His first Parliament reveals far-reaching reform plans.

Chamberlain's financial duties transferred to Treasurer and Comptroller.

The Crown claims rights to all mining of gold and silver.

Representatives of impoverished litigants (Advocates for the Poor) are to be reimbursed from public funds.

Completion of St Machar's Cathedral, Aberdeen.

1425

Fall of the Albany Stewarts. Murdoch, Duke of Albany, beheaded at Stirling.

Disputes with the Papacy begin.

Sir Walter Ogilvy is first Treasurer; David Brown, chancellor of Glasgow Cathedral, is first Comptroller.

James I founds Charterhouse at Perth, last Scottish monastery to be established. He warns the clergy against a decline in standards.

1426

All laws other than the King's are abolished.

1428

James I visits Inverness; action against the Highland chiefs includes executions and imprisonment.

1429

Submission of the Lord of the Isles.

1430

Bishopric of the Isles established.

Sumptuary laws passed for restraint in dress. Persons found
    playing football to be fined fourpence.

1431

Battle of Inverlochy: Donald Balloch defeats royal army.

Bubonic plague in Edinburgh and again in 1432.

1433

A Hussite heretic burned at the stake in St Andrews.

1434

Prolonged severe winter weather this year and next causes
    hardship.

1435

Aeneas Sylvius Piccolomini, the future Pope Pius II, visits
    Scotland as a papal ambassador.

1436

James I fails to take Roxburgh Castle.

1437

Assassination of James I at Perth (21 February). Accession of
    James II.

1438

Warfare breaks out among the nobility.

A plague year, continued in 1439.

1439

Sir William Crichton appointed Chancellor.

Battle of Craignaucht Hill between factions of the Boyds and
    Stewarts.

1440

William, Earl of Douglas, and his brother executed after Black
    Dinner of the Douglases (24 November).

1442

Bishops dispute in the 'Little Schism'.

1444

Deposition of Chancellor Crichton.

1445

Garde Ecossaise formed as senior company of French Household Troops.

1446

Warfare between Ogilvies and Lindsays.

1447

Loch Fyne herring industry thriving: it produces 'in mair plenti than ony seas of Albion.'

1448

English raid Annandale and burn Dumfries; thrown back by Hugh Douglas, Earl of Ormond (23 October).

Franco-Scottish alliance renewed at Tours (31 December).

1449

Marriage of James II to Mary of Gueldres (3 July).

Post of Admiral of Scotland is introduced.

Death of Walter Bower, author of the continuation of the *Scotichronicon*.

1450

Fall of the Livingstons.

James II grants Glasgow Green to the town of Glasgow.

Around now Gypsies enter the south of Scotland.

1451

University of Glasgow founded by Bishop Turnbull.

1452

Murder of the Earl of Douglas by James II in Stirling Castle (22 February).

1453

Richard Holland composes *The Buke of the Howlat* for Archibald Douglas, Earl of Moray.

John Crukshanks is paid 30 shillings a year to maintain the common clocks of Aberdeen.

1454

Parliament encourages landowners to plant trees and hedges.

1455

Act of Annexation defines the Crown's sources of finance.

Final defeat of Black Douglases at Arkinholm (June).

1456

Around this time Sir Gilbert Hay translates *The Buke of the Law of Armys*, from French, for William Sinclair, Earl of Orkney: the first literary prose in Scots.

1457

Parliament again tries without success to ban football, also golf.

Parliament encourages tenancy under feu-farm.

1460

Accidental death of James II in siege of Roxburgh Castle. Accession of James III.

1461

Berwick retaken from England.

Book of Pluscarden compiled, containing much current information.

1462

The Lord of the Isles makes Treaty of Ardtornish (13 February) with Edward IV of England and the Earl of Douglas, for the partition of Scotland.

The poet Robert Henryson recorded as graduating in Glasgow University.

1466

Boyds and Kennedies rise to power as 'tutors' of the king.
The coining of copper 'black money' tried and discontinued.
From now parliament keeps its own records, separate from the
    king's council.

1468

The pledging of Orkney and Shetland.
Marriage of James III to Margaret of Denmark.

1469

Parliamentary commission set up to review and codify the law.
Burgh elections regulated. The old council to select the new one.

1471

Preparations made against English invasion.
Collegiate Church of St Duthac established at Tain.
Burghs and lords encouraged to build fishing boats to catch
    herring.

1472

Formal annexation of Orkney and Shetland.
James III proposes to enforce his claim to be also Duke of
    Brittany. Fall of the Boyds from power.
St Andrews raised to archbishopric.

1473

Parliament deplores the lack of gold and coin in the country.
Edinburgh hatmakers form a craft guild.

1474

Marriage treaty and truce with England.
Laws passed to promote sea fishing.
Town councils ordered to set up schools for musical
    education. These co-exist for a time with the grammar
    schools.
Edinburgh skinners form a craft guild.

1476

Submission of Lord of the Isles: Earldom of Ross annexed to the Crown.

James III grants a three-year safe-conduct to Florentine merchants.

1478

Serious feuding and fighting in Angus, Sutherland and Caithness.

Office of King's Advocate established (later Lord Advocate).

'Blind Harry's' *Wallace* appears.

1479

Parliament (March) records trouble and fighting in many parts of the kingdom.

Duke of Albany imprisoned in Edinburgh Castle, escapes to France.

1480

Battle between MacDonalds and Mackenzies in Wester Ross.

1481

War with England.

Internecine strife in the Western Isles: Battle of the Bloody Bay.

1482

James III's favourites murdered by the barons at Lauder. Temporary imprisonment of James III. Richard of Gloucester enters Edinburgh. Final loss of Berwick to England. Return of Albany.

Debasement of coinage raises prices and heightens scarcity of food and goods.

1483

James III restored to power. Flight of Duke of Albany (May).

1485

Assay office known to be functioning in Edinburgh.

Existence of a grammar school in Brechin is recorded.

1486

Leith Academy is founded around this year.

1487

Warfare in the far north between the Rosses and Mackays.

1488

Rebellion against James III. Battle of Sauchieburn. Death of James III. Accession of James IV.

1489

Fighting at sea between Sir Andrew Wood's vessels and English vessels.

c. 1490

Rebellions against James IV put down.

Drummonds burn 120 Murrays to death in church of Monzievaird.

The composer, Robert Carver, writes church music for the Chapel Royal, Stirling.

Provision made for building a grammar school in Elgin.

1491

Alliance with Denmark renewed.

Bands and convocations within the burghs are forbidden.

1492

Glasgow raised to archbishopric.

1493

Lord of the Isles forfeited: his domains go to the Crown.

1494

James IV cruises up the west coast.

First reference in the Exchequer rolls to the production of whisky.

1495

The English Pretender, Perkin Warbeck, welcomed in Scotland.

University of Aberdeen founded by Bishop Elphinstone.

1496

Don Pedro de Ayala reports to Spain on conditions in Scotland.

Education Act passed: barons and freeholders to send their eldest sons to grammar schools.

1497

Venereal disease reaches Scotland; closure of brothels ordered in Aberdeen.

1498

James IV holds court at Kilkerran (later Campbeltown).

Plague attacks afflict the towns.

Shore Porters' Society founded or re-founded in Aberdeen.

First mention of coal mining at Machrihanish in Kintyre.

1500

Population estimated at around 500,000.

Earl of Argyll becomes King's Lieutenant in the west.

King's College Chapel, Aberdeen, begun (till 1504). Iona Abbey rebuilding completed: raised to cathedral status.

William Dunbar (*c.*1460–*c.*1520) is appointed court poet.

Knitting is introduced to Shetland from the mainland.

1501

Earl of Huntly becomes King's Lieutenant in the north.

James IV begins building of Palace of Holyrood in Edinburgh.

1502

Death of James IV's mistress, Margaret Drummond, and her sisters, after a suspect breakfast.

1503

Marriage of James IV to Margaret Tudor (8 August).

William Dunbar composes *The Thrissil and the Rois*.

1504

Rising of Donald Dubh in the Western Isles (until 1507).

Sir Andrew Wood captures three English ships off Dundee.

1505

College of Surgeons and its Library established in Edinburgh.
Guild of Barber-Surgeons given a monopoly on whisky production.

1506

Commissioners appointed to 'compose' feuds in the Western Isles.
Building of the ship *Great Michael*.

1507

Introduction of the printing press by Andrew Myllar and Walter Chepman. Dunbar's *Poems* one of the first books to be printed.

1508

Annual royal audits held at Edinburgh from now on.
Earl of Huntly appointed hereditary sheriff at Inverness, with mandate to enforce peace in the Highlands.
Scottish ships sent to the Baltic to support the King of Denmark.
William Dunbar publishes *Lament for the Makaris*.

1509

James IV ceases to hold parliaments.
Bishop Elphinstone's *Aberdeen Breviary*, lists 70 Scottish saints. It provides a liturgy for Scotland, replacing the Sarum liturgy.

1510

James IV proposes a new Crusade.
First curling club recorded at Kilsyth.
First record of gooseberries, grown as hedgerow bushes in the Dundee area.
Around this time, Jean Damian tries flying from the walls of Stirling Castle (unsuccessfully).

1512

Book of the Dean of Lismore compiled (until 1526): an anthology of Gaelic verse.

1513

Birth of John Knox (dies 1572).

French appeal for Scottish assistance against Henry VIII. Scottish ships bombard Carrickfergus.

Battle of Flodden (9 September): defeat of the Scots by English army under the Earl of Surrey, with an estimated 10,000 dead, including King James IV.

Accession of James V.

Small quantities of gold mined at Crawford Muir.

1515

Regency of the Duke of Albany commences.

Gavin Douglas (*c.*1474–1522), poet and translator of the *Aeneid*, becomes Bishop of Dunkeld: has to fight his way in against an opposing faction.

1517

Treaty of Rouen, renewing the French alliance.

1518

Serious clan fighting between now and 1522 in Sutherland, among Gunns, Sutherlands, Mackays and Murrays.

1520

'Cleanse the Causey' battle in Edinburgh.

Murdoch Nisbet makes a version of Wycliffe's *New Testament* in Scots. This is not published until the 19th century.

Completion of St Machar's Cathedral, Aberdeen.

1521

Alexander MacDonald of Islay takes an army into Ulster in support of O'Donnell against the English.

John Major (*c.*1470–1550) publishes his *Historia Majoris Britanniae*.

1524

Scotland is effectively ruled by the 'Red Douglas', Earl of Angus.

1526

Hector Boece's (*c.*1465–1536) *Historia Gentis Scotorum* published.

Right of mining gold and silver leased to a group of Germans and Dutchmen.

1527

Hector MacIntosh burns 24 Ogilvies to death in their own castle.

Bridge of Dee built, Aberdeen.

Barry Links recorded as a golfing site.

1528

James V escapes from tutelage of the Earl of Angus: downfall of Douglas rule.

The sheriffs of the north instructed to destroy Chattan clan.

Patrick Hamilton, Protestant martyr, burned at St Andrews (29 February).

1529

Sir David Lyndsay's *Complaynt to the King* published.

1530

Hanging of Johnnie Armstrong and other Border freebooters at the order of James V.

1532

Robert Henryson publishes *The Testament of Cresseid*.

Inauguration of the College of Justice, or Court of Session. First president is Walter Mylne, Abbot of Cambuskenneth.

Origin of the Faculty of Advocates.

North Sea fishery 'war' with the Dutch until 1541.

1533

English officials in Ireland complain about increase of Scots in Ulster.

Beginning of the Convention of Royal Burghs.

1534

A new Treaty of Perpetual Peace between Scotland and England signed.

1535

Parliament attempts to stop the landowners imposing themselves on the burghs as provosts and bailies and profiteering from their positions.

1536

James V visits France to marry the daughter of Francis I; she dies shortly after arriving in Scotland.

John Bellenden publishes *Chroniklis of Scotland*, an English version of Boece's *Historia Gentis Scotorum*.

1539

A real tennis court is built at Falkland Palace.

1540

James V sails round the north and west.

James V recognizes the Gypsy kingdom of 'John Faw, lord and erle of Little Egypt', and allows his laws to appertain to his people.

Sir David Lyndsay publishes *Ane Pleasant Satyre of The Thrie Estaitis*.

John Mosman of Edinburgh makes the still extant crown for James V.

1541

James V fails to meet Henry VIII in York.

Campveere recognized as sole Scottish staple port of the Netherlands.

Salaries for judges introduced.

1542

English fleet harries Scottish shipping. Battle of Solway Moss (November): English army defeats Scots led by Oliver Sinclair.

Death of James V. Accession of Mary I (later Mary, Queen of Scots) at the age of one week. Regency of Earl of Arran.

Around now the *Black Book of Paisley* is written, containing a text of the *Scotichronicon*, etc.

The palace within Stirling Castle is completed.

1543

Treaty of Greenwich (July) provides for Mary's marriage to Prince Edward of England.

An Act is passed for publication of the Bible 'in Inglis or Scottis' – not carried out (15 March).

The Setons begin Seton Palace, perhaps the first Scottish 'country mansion'.

1544

English occupy and sack Edinburgh in Henry VIII's 'rough wooing' of Mary I for his son.

Isle of Arran devastated by an English fleet under the command of the Earl of Lennox.

Battle of *Blair-na-Leine* (Field of Shirts) in the Great Glen, between the Frasers and Clanranald MacDonalds.

1545

Scots under Arran defeat the English at the Battle of Ancrum Moor (February).

1546

Burning of George Wishart, Protestant martyr, in St Andrews (1 March).

Murder of Cardinal Beaton in St Andrews Castle (May).

1547

Battle of Pinkie (10 September). 'Black Saturday' (30 July): St Andrews Castle surrendered to French troops. John Knox exiled.

1548

Mary, Queen of Scots, is sent to France for her protection (August).

1549

John Knox publishes *Epistle on Justification by Faith*.

1549

Donald Monro publishes *A Description of the Western Islands*.
Many Hebridean mercenaries engaged in fighting for the Irish
against English supremacy.

1550

The Complaynt of Scotland published in Paris.
From about now until 1700 a comparatively colder weather
period sets in, sometimes referred to as 'the little Ice Age'.

1551

Frequent raids by the West Highlanders on the Irish coast.

1552

Convention of Royal Burghs enacts that all burghs shall model
their government on that of Edinburgh.
First mention of golf being played at St Andrews.

1553

Gavin Douglas's translation of the *Aeneid* and his poem 'The
Palice of Honour' are published.

1554

Mary of Guise becomes Regent.

1555

John Knox prompts Lord James Stewart to form the band of
'Lords of the Congregation'.
The 'Bloody Vespers' of Elgin (1 January): a battle in the
cathedral between followers of William Innes and Alexander
Dunbar.

1557

Signing of the first Covenant (3 December).

1558

The English deputy in Ireland, the Earl of Sussex, carries out
reprisal raids on the west coast.

Marriage of Mary I to the Dauphin Francis.

Walter Mylne burned to death at St Andrews, the last pre-Reformation martyr (28 April).

Knox publishes *First Blast of the Trumpet Against the Monstrous Regiment of Women*.

1559

John Knox returns to Scotland.

Stripping of churches begins in Perth.

Reformers take over Edinburgh; Mary of Guise retreats to Leith.

Wars of religion begin.

1560

Siege of Leith and departure of the French. Treaty of Edinburgh establishes Protestant dominance. Death of Mary of Guise.

The Reformation Parliament. Fall of the Catholic Church.

Establishment of the General Assembly of the Kirk (20 December). Publication of the *Book of Discipline*. Publication of the Geneva Bible.

Around this time, Robert Lindsay of Pitscottie was writing his *Historie and Cronicles of Scotland*, which was not published until 1778.

1561

Mary, Queen of Scots returns to Scotland (19 August).

Protestant Confession of Faith drawn up.

Rioting in Edinburgh when magistrates enforce a ban on the Robin Hood pageant.

1562

Mary I rides to Inverness and Aberdeen; power of the Earl of Huntly broken.

Ninian Winzet (1518–92) writes *Certane Tractatis for Reformatioun of Doctryne and Maneris*: a tract against Protestantism but in favour of reform.

1563

Lead mining is licensed to two Edinburgh burgesses.

1563

Witchcraft made a civil crime.

Bad harvest pushes up the cost of meal, with consequent hardship.

1564

First Scottish *Psalter* printed.

First mention of Fair Isle as a producer of coarse stockings.

1565

Marriage of Mary I to Lord Darnley. The Chaseabout Raid ensues.

Bad harvest causes food shortage, and again in 1567.

1566

Murder of David Riccio in Holyrood Palace (March).

Birth of the future James VI (June).

Privy Council orders that 'nane molest the Hielandmen' coming to Lowland markets.

1567

Murder of Darnley (9 February). Mary I marries Earl of Bothwell. Deposition of Mary. Accession of James VI. Regency of Earl of Moray.

First book printed in Gaelic: translation of John Knox's *Liturgy*.

1568

Escape of Mary I from Loch Leven. Battle of Langside (14 May). Escape and flight to England of Mary (19 May).

George Bannatyne publishes the *Ballat Buik*.

Death of Robert Carver, court composer (born *c.*1484).

1569

Around now, the Scots College in Paris is established by Archbishop James Beaton.

1570

Assassination of the Regent Moray. George Buchanan (1506–82), leading humanist, appointed tutor to the King.

Meat eating banned during Lent for 'the commoun weill'.

1571

Wars of religion. The 'King's Lords' besiege Edinburgh Castle, held by the 'Queen's Lords'. The Archbishop of St Andrews is hanged, in Stirling.

1572

Regency of Earl of Morton.

Death of John Knox.

Bad harvest makes a year of scarcity and high meal prices.

1573

Edinburgh Castle surrendered, almost destroyed (29 May). Death of Maitland of Lethington and hanging of Kirkcaldy of Grange, the castle's defenders.

Because of shortage, export of salt forbidden, except in ships that had brought in timber.

1575

Unauthorized beggars to be scourged and branded, by an Act of Parliament.

1576

Fighting breaks out during a race meeting at Ayr.

1577

Three hundred and ninety MacDonalds are suffocated in a cave on Eigg, by the MacLeods.

Glasgow University is reformed in a 'Novo Erectio'.

1578

James VI assumes government.

Confirmation of privileges of Convention of Royal Burghs. Staple port at Campveere confirmed again.

1579

Arrival in Scotland of Esmé Stewart, soon to be Duke of Lennox.

Shortage of barley: whisky-making restricted to earls, lords, barons and gentlemen, for their own use.

1580

Merchants are forbidden to change nationality to benefit their business.
First Bible printed in Scotland, purchase price £4 13/4d.
Song schools made a burgh rather than a church responsibility.

1580

East coast fishermen begin about now to fish the Minch.

1581

Fall and execution of the Regent Morton.
James VI publishes the *Negative Confession*, an attack on Catholicism, to mollify Protestants.
Islesmen continue to raid Ulster. Orkney Earldom and Bishopric under Earl Robert Stewart.
Inchcolm Island noted as a den of pirates.

1582

The Ruthven Raid: attempt to hold James VI hostage.
Constant feuding between the Mackenzies and the Glengarry MacDonalds.
Foundation of Edinburgh University.
Publication of George Buchanan's *Rerum Scoticarum Historia*.

1584

The 'Black Acts' enforce the King's superiority over the Kirk.
Outbreaks of bubonic plague.

*c.***1585**

Death of 'The Admirable Crichton'.

1586

Battle of Ardnary in Ireland: invading Highlanders defeated.
In Sutherland, violent warfare between Mackays, Sutherlands, Gunns and Sinclairs.

1587

Execution in England of Mary, Queen of Scots (8 February).
Act of Annexation: the Crown takes over ecclesiastical holdings.

54

Act passed for 'the quieting and keeping in obedience of the disorderit subjectis inhabitant of the Borders, Highlands and Isles'.

Reforms to Court of Session.

Export of foodstuffs prohibited because of shortages.

1588

Ships of the Spanish Armada driven north round Scotland by storms; some are wrecked, including one in Tobermory Bay.

1589

James VI marries Anne of Denmark. Leaves country for 6 months.

Six hundred Islesmen raid County Mayo.

The High Kirk Session of Glasgow bans golf and shinty on Sundays and working days.

1590

Witchcraft trial in North Berwick: witches suspected of making spells against the King.

1592

Presbyterianism established by the 'Golden Act'.

Murder of the 'bonnie' Earl of Moray.

Parliament bans export of sheep and cattle because of food shortages.

1593

Founding of Marischal College, Aberdeen.

1594

Battle of Glenlivet: Earl of Huntly defeats Earl of Argyll (3 October).

Parliament complains about the wild behaviour of university students and teachers.

Chair of Law set up at Edinburgh University.

Building of Provost Ross's House, Aberdeen.

1595

Archibald Napier publishes *The New Order of Gooding and Manuring of All Sorts of Field Land with Common Salts.*

1596

Boys at Edinburgh High School mutiny, and shoot Bailie John McMorran.

A famine year, with grain imports, high prices, and hardship among the poor.

1596

Re-enactment of the 'Black Acts.'

Appointment of eight Commissioners, 'the Octavians', to supervise the exchequer.

Northern earls submit to James VI.

Rescue of Kinmont Willie from Carlisle Castle by Walter Scott.

Dysart and Culross fined £100 each for illegally exporting coal.

1597

Import duty levied for the first time, at one shilling in the pound.

Plantation of Lewis by 'Fife Adventurers' begins.

Landholders in the Highlands and Islands ordered to produce charters or evidence of their territorial rights.

James VI publishes *Demonologie*, a book on witchcraft.

1598

General Assembly agrees bishops may sit in Parliament.

James VI publishes *Basilikon Doron*, a book on monarchy.

Feuds between MacDonalds and Macleans cause bloodshed in the Western Isles.

Whisky listed among other exports to Ireland.

Fynes Morison, an English traveller, notes that the Scots gentry use 'no Art of Cookery'.

1599

Complaints about conduct of Earl of Orkney include piracy.

Faculty of Physicians and Surgeons established in Glasgow.

1600

First day of the New Year is moved this year to 1 January; previously on Lady Day, 25 March.

The Gowrie Conspiracy.

Bishops restored to the Church of Scotland.

Scots College established in Rome.

Privy Council licenses 100 foreign clothworkers to enter the
country on advantageous terms, to pass on their skills.

1601

Tax levied on wine 'to restrain drunkenness'.

Feud on Skye between MacLeods and MacDonalds
culminates in the Battle of Bencoullen.

1603

James VI becomes also James I of England in the Union of the
Crowns, and leaves Edinburgh for London.

Massacre by Clanranald MacDonalds of Mackenzies, by fire
whilst at worship in the church of Kilchrist .

1604

First commission for a Treaty of Union between Scotland and
England.

Famine in the Highlands.

Earls of Argyll and Atholl combine to attack the proscribed
Clan MacGregor.

1605

James VI sets up a Border Commission to enforce peace in the
Border country.

1606

Act of Parliament allows for serfdom of coal and salt workers
as 'necessary servants'.

1607

English Parliament rejects union with Scotland.

Earl Patrick's palace built in Kirkwall, Orkney.

1608

Plantation of Ulster begins. Many people move there from the
Border country.

1609

The Statutes of Icolmkill.

Plantation of Lewis abandoned.

James VI acknowledges the status of the Beatons or MacBeths as physicians in the Isles.

Justices of the Peace established around this time.

Salt panning established on a large scale along the East Lothian coastline.

1610

Proscription of the MacGregors renewed.

1611

Publication of the *Authorized Version of the Bible*.

Glasgow receives charter as royal burgh.

1612

Parliament grants a patent for the manufacture of sulphur and chemicals.

1614

John Napier of Merchiston (1550–1617) publishes *Mirifici Logarithmorum Canonis Descriptio*, first work on logarithms.

Coal exports run at around 14,000 tons, mostly to the Netherlands.

1615

Earl of Caithness arrests Earl of Orkney on Privy Council orders. Execution of Earl of Orkney.

Great unrest in Kintyre and Islay with the rebellion of Sir James MacDonald. Crown forces brought from Ireland and Scotland.

Hanging of John Ogilvie (canonized in 1976) for refusing to deny supremacy of the Pope .

1616

An Act of Council proposes the establishment of parish schools.

Local warfare endemic in the far north, between Earls of Caithness and Sutherland.

Chiefs are instructed to send their sons to Lowland schools, and to keep only one galley.

Status of Campveere as Scottish staple port reaffirmed.

William Drummond of Hawthornden publishes his *Poems*.

1617

James VI revisits Edinburgh (May). He presents Dumfries with 'Silver Gun of the Seven Trades' as a shooting trophy.

1618

The Five Articles of Perth are promulgated.

Coal mines at Culross extend beneath the sea.

Matthew Taylor, the 'Water Poet', visits Scotland.

1619

First slate-roofed buildings in Sutherland.

1620

Erection of Gladstone's Land, tall tenement in Edinburgh.

George Jamesone (*c.*1588–1644), first recorded Scottish portraitist, active in Aberdeen.

1621

Sir William Alexander receives charter for the establishment of Nova Scotia (29 September).

Nathaniel Udwort of Edinburgh purchases a monopoly on soap-making.

1623

Failed harvest produces much hardship and many deaths.

1624

The Privy Council threatens sanctions against those who visit 'Christ's Well' at Doune.

Death of George Heriot (born 1563), goldsmith and money-lender to the King: 'Jingling Geordie'.

1625

Death of James VI. Accession of Charles I.

Judges removed from Privy Council, to concentrate on Court of Session work.

1627

A commission of inquiry reveals many parishes without school or schoolmaster.

1628

Building of George Heriot's Hospital (now School), until 1659.

1630

Numerous witchcraft trials during this time.

1631

Earl of Stirling (Sir William Alexander) given monopoly on copper farthings.

1632

Nova Scotia colonists forced out by the French.

Construction of Parliament House in Edinburgh begins, until 1640.

1633

Coronation in Edinburgh of Charles I. Act passed for the establishment of a school in every parish.

Formation of a corps by Sir John Hepburn, to become the Royal Scots.

1635

Scottish mercenary officers and soldiers begin returning from the Continent.

First inland postal service, between Edinburgh and London.

Proposal made to erect a lighthouse on the Isle of May (first in Scotland).

A 'snorting and dowking' sea monster sighted off Aberdeen (July).

1637

Promulgation of the new *Scottish Prayer Book* creates social disorder (23 July).

1638

Signing of the National Covenant (28 February). General Assembly abolishes bishops (November-December).

William Lithgow (*c*.1582–*c*.1650) publishes his *Totall Discourse of Rare Adventures and Painfull Peregrinations...from Scotland*.

1639

The first Bishops' War, and Pacification of Berwick.

The Trot of Turriff (14 May): Royalists scatter a Covenanting force.

1640

The second Bishops' War. Scots occupy Newcastle. Harrying of Catholic clans by Argyll; burning of 'the bonny hoose of Airlie'. Montrose makes the Cumbernauld Bond against Argyll.

The Wedderburn brothers publish the *Gude and Godlie Ballatis* around this time.

1641

Charles I visits Edinburgh in the hope of making allies.

1642

Founding of the Scots Guards (28 March).

1643

The Solemn League and Covenant made with the English Parliament (13 October).

The Westminster Assembly of Divines promulgates a Confession of Faith, Larger and Shorter Catechisms, etc.

1644

Scots invade England.

Siege of Newcastle and Battle of Marston Moor.

Montrose named King's Lieutenant in Scotland. Campaigns of Montrose begin. Montrose's victory at Tippermuir (1 September).

Parliament introduces excise duty of 2/8d per pint on whisky.

Outbreaks of bubonic plague frequent between now and 1649. Around a quarter of Edinburgh's population die in this outbreak.

1645

Montrose's victories at Inverlochy (2 February); Auldearn (9 May); Alford (2 July); Kilsyth (15 August); captures Edinburgh in August; defeated at Philiphaugh (13 September).

1646

Charles I surrenders himself to the Scots army (5 May).

1647

Charles I handed over to the English Parliament (30 January). The Engagement made: a treaty between Charles I and certain lords.

1648

Battle of Preston (17 July). Cromwell defeats the Engagers.

Cromwell in Scotland.

The 'Whiggamore Raid' on Edinburgh: extreme Presbyterians take over government.

1649

Execution of Charles I (30 January). Accession of Charles II; his proclamation in Edinburgh.

Last visitations of bubonic plague.

1650

Battle of Carbisdale (27 April). Capture and execution (21 May) of Montrose. Charles II lands in Scotland (June). Battle of Dunbar (2 September): Cromwell defeats Scots army.

Introduction of Metric Psalms.

Famine in the Highlands.

1651

Battle of Inverkeithing (2 July): Royalists defeated by Cromwellian army.

Battle of Worcester (3 September): Charles II's army defeated by Cromwell.

Dundee sacked by General Monk.

Scotland is brought under Cromwellian rule.

Mercurius Scoticus, first Scottish newspaper, published in Leith; later banned.

1652

The Scottish regalia hidden from Cromwell's troopers by James Granger, minister of Kinneff.

English–Dutch war disrupts Scots–Dutch trade, until 1654.

Thirty Scots members sent to join the Protectorate Parliament in London.

1653

Scotland formally unified with England and Ireland under the Commonwealth.

Sir Thomas Urquhart (*c.*1611–60) publishes the first two books of his translation of Rabelais.

1654

General Monk defeats Royalists under Middleton at Dalnaspidal.

The Camerons are the last of the clans formally to submit to Cromwellian rule.

Dundee offers free entry to merchants' guild, to combat the dearth of men and trade in the town.

1656

Justices of the Peace for Midlothian draw up pay scales for four separate grades of farm servant.

1658

'Physic Garden' established at Surgeon's House, Edinburgh: a forerunner of the Royal Botanic Gardens.

1658

Oliver Cromwell claims to have freed 'the meaner sort' of Scots from the 'great lords'.

1660

Restoration of Charles II.

Oldest extant portrait of a figure in the belted plaid.

From now on the importing of tea and coffee becomes significant. Coffee houses begin to open in Edinburgh.

1661

The Drunken Parliament annuls all Presbyterian legislation. Restoration of episcopacy. James Sharp appointed Archbishop of St Andrews.

Execution of Marquis of Argyll.

Ship *Elizabeth* is wrecked carrying state papers being returned from England to Scotland (18 December).

1662

Acts are passed to discourage wine drinking in the Western Isles, thereby stimulating whisky-making, and against the use of Gaelic as a 'barbarous' language.

Restoration of lay patronage.

Forbes' *Songs and Fancies* published in Aberdeen – first secular music published in Scotland.

1663

Expulsion of non-conforming ministers. Holding of Conventicles begins.

1664

Lime trees first planted in Scotland, at Taymouth.

1665

English–Dutch war again disrupts Scots–Dutch trade, until 1667.

1666

The Pentland Rising (November). Galloway Covenanters are scattered at the Battle of Rullion Green (26 November).

1667

Commissioners of Supply are appointed in the shires.

Glasgow creates a deep sea-going port at Port Glasgow.

Twice-weekly postal service between Edinburgh and Aberdeen.

1669

Charles II's first Letter of Indulgence. Duke of Lauderdale fails to bring about a union of the Parliaments.

1670

Founding of Royal Company for the Fishery of Scotland.

Forth coal mines estimated to yield around 50,000 tons of coal a year.

1671

High Court of Justiciary established as central criminal court.

1672

Parliament reduces the monopoly powers of royal burghs.

Charles II's second Letter of Indulgence.

Lyon Office established as central armorial registry.

English–Dutch war again disrupts Scots–Dutch trade. Philip van der Straten, of Flanders, starts up the woollen industry of the Borders, at Kelso.

Early mention of turnips, recorded as stolen from fields, in records of Baron Court of Urie.

1674

Heavy winter snow kills many cattle in the Borders.

1675

First paper-works in Scotland, at Dalry.

1676

Royal Company of Archers set up as sovereign's bodyguard.

1677

Battle between two Gypsy tribes, Faas and Shaws, at Romanno Bridge (1 October).

1678

Duke of Lauderdale sends Highlanders to pacify Ayrshire.

David Calderwood (1575–1651) publishes *History of the Church of Scotland*.

Earl of Mar raises a regiment, later to become the Royal Scots Fusiliers (23 September).

1679

Murder of Archbishop Sharp (May).

Battles of Drumclog (May) and Bothwell Brig (June).

Duke of York becomes Commissioner in Scotland.

Rebuilding of Holyrood Palace completed.

Earliest recorded pipe major in the army: Alexander Wallace of Dumbarton's Regiment.

1680

Cameronians defeated by dragoons at Airds Moss (22 July). Death of Richard Cameron.

1681

The 'Test' imposed, following passing of the Test Act.

Edinburgh Assay Office begins to use letters to indicate dates.

General Tam Dalyell raises a regiment, Royal Regiment of Scots Dragoons, later Royal Scots Greys (25 November).

Viscount Stair (1619–95) publishes *Institutes of the Law in Scotland*, first full codification of Scots Law.

The Royal College of Physicians founded by Sir Robert Sibbald.

Annual wine import estimated at 1,600 tuns.

1682

Advocates' Library, Edinburgh, founded (now National Library).

1683

Hearth Tax introduced.

First Scots gardening book, John Reid's *The Scots Gardiner*.

1684

Start of the 'Killing Time'. Covenanters risk being shot out of hand. *The Apologetical Declaration* by James Renwick threatens death to anyone acting against the Cameronians.

The Dutch artist, de Witt, is hired to paint the kings of Scotland, from his imagination, for £250, to decorate Holyrood Palace.

1685

Death of Charles II. Accession of James VII.

Failed invasion by the Earl of Argyll results in his execution.

Two women Covenanters are drowned at Wigtown (11 May).

The Gaelic bard, Iain Lom (*c.*1624–*c.*1710), visits the court of Charles II.

1686

James VII's first Letter of Indulgence.

1687

James VII's second Letter of Indulgence.

1688

James VII's third Letter of Indulgence.

Flight of James VII to France.

Establishment of William II and Mary II in London.

French wars with England have adverse affect on Scottish trade with France, until 1697.

Central tower of St Machar's Cathedral, Aberdeen, falls in.

Poor harvest and starvation on Skye.

1689

Parliament deposes James VII (March) and claims the right to choose the monarch.

William and Mary confirmed as joint sovereigns.

Earl of Leven raises a Border regiment, later the King's Own Scottish Borderers (18 March). Earl of Angus forms the Cameronians into a regiment (19 April).

Battle of Killiekrankie (27 July), high point of the Jacobite Rising orchestrated by John Graham of Claverhouse, Viscount Dundee (born 1648), who is killed in the process.

Cameronians hold Dunkeld against the Highlanders.

MacDonalds of Keppoch defeat the MacIntoshes in one of the last inter-clan battles.

Ferintosh Distillery, near Dingwall, first bulk producer of whisky, burned down by supporters of James VII.

1690

Presbyterianism established as form of church in Scotland.

Royal supremacy over the church abolished.

Parliament passes first of numerous Acts for the Observation of the Sabbath.

Jacobite forces defeated in Battle of Cromdale (1 May).

Reverend Robert Kirk has his translation of the Bible into Gaelic printed in London.

First rope works in Scotland, in Glasgow.

Maple and walnut trees first planted in Scotland.

1691

Convention of Royal Burghs enquires as to the state of the royal burghs, revealing serious reduction in trade and activity generally.

Jacobites imprisoned on Bass Rock capture it in James VII's name.

1692

Massacre of Glencoe (13 February).

Death of Robert Kirk, minister of Aberfoyle, author of *The Secret Commonwealth of Elves, Faunes and Fairies* and translator of the Bible into Gaelic.

1693

MacGregor name proscribed again.

First public music concerts in Edinburgh.

John Slezer publishes his *Theatrum Scotiae*, views of Scottish towns.

1694

Death of Mary II. Solo reign of William III.

Bass Rock recaptured from Jacobite rebels.

William Paterson (1658–1719) founds Bank of England.

Act to support linen manufacture: all shrouds to be made of plain linen.

1695

Company of Scotland Trading to Africa and the Indies founded.

Bank of Scotland founded.

Martin Martin publishes *Description of the Western Islands of Scotland*.

First public concert given in Edinburgh.

A General Post Office is set up in Edinburgh.

Poor and late harvest causes hardship.

The potato recorded as being cultivated in Scotland and the Western Isles.

1696

Education Act prescribes a school in every parish (*see* 1633).

Another failed harvest causes much hardship. Duties lifted on virtually all food imports.

1697

Paisley witch trials.

Thomas Aikenhead, aged 19, hanged in Edinburgh for blasphemy and his corpse burned.

Records include mention of red and white varieties of potato.

1698

The Darien colonial venture is launched. Three ships leave on 1 July; two others follow later.

Harvest fails again, causing starvation and deaths. Andrew Fletcher estimates the number of beggars at 200,000.

1699

Grain export forbidden because of the shortage.

A woollen manufactory is established in Glasgow.

1700

Population estimated at around 1,000,000; only 200 on St Kilda.

News comes of the collapse and abandoning of the Darien colonial venture.

James Macpherson, bandit and fiddle player, hanged at Banff.

Salt panning consumes an estimated 150,000 tons of coal a year, and produces 25,000 tons of salt.

Great fire in Edinburgh destroys many buildings around Parliament House.

1702

Death of William III. Accession of Anne.

Commissioners appointed to draft Treaty of Union; talks collapse.

Further English–French war disrupts trade with France.

1703

Scottish Parliament passes Act of Security.

John Adair publishes *Description of the Sea-Coast and Islands of Scotland*.

Three women are scourged in the regality of Grant for bringing whisky to two men condemned to hang.

1704

Dunkeld is last royal burgh to receive a charter.

Alexander Selkirk is put ashore on Juan Fernandez: prototype of 'Robinson Crusoe'.

1705

English Parliament passes Aliens Act against Scots.

The *Worcester* incident (hanging of English seamen at Leith) brings to a peak the hostile feeling between England and Scotland.

Linen Act of 1694 repealed: shrouds must now be of wool, to protect the woollen industry.

1706

Treaty of Union is drawn up in London and presented to Parliament in Edinburgh.

1707

Act of Union formally passed (16 January). Dissolution of the Scottish Parliament (April) and formation of the United Kingdom Parliament (1May).

Customs and Excise Service established in Scotland.

1708

Abolition of the Scottish Privy Council.

Edinburgh University first to abolish the 'regent' system of teaching.

1709

The Kirk sets up Society for the Propagation of Christian Knowledge, for education in the Highlands and Islands. General Assembly recommends a library in each presbytery.

Prolonged bad weather causes bad harvest and much hardship.

1710

Dancing 'assemblies' begin in Edinburgh.

Large-scale building of dry-stone dykes in Galloway to enclose land.

1711

Export duty imposed on linen industry.

Birth of David Hume, the philospher (dies 1776).

1712

Central tower of Elgin Cathedral collapses.

1712

Patronage Act: lay patronage of church ministers restored.

Parliament attempts to increase Malt Tax: prevented by protests of Scottish members.

1714

Death of Anne. Accession of George I.

Catholic seminary set up by Loch Morar.

1715

Jacobite Rising under the Earl of Mar. Jacobites take Perth. Battle of Sheriffmuir (13 November).

Horse-borne post introduced between Edinburgh and Glasgow.

1716

The Old Pretender lands at Peterhead (January) and leaves from Montrose (February). End of the 1715-16 Jacobite Rising.

Disarming Acts passed.

1717

Horse-borne post introduced from Glasgow to Edinburgh and north.

1718

Glasgow and Greenock owned vessels regularly cross the Atlantic, engaging in slave traffic as well as in goods.

1719

Battle of Glenshiel (10 June); Jacobites and Spanish allies defeated. Eilan Donan Castle demolished by naval gunnery.

Allan Ramsay (1686–1758) sets up as a bookseller in Edinburgh, begins to publish his poetry.

1720

First steam pumping engine in a Scottish coal mine, at Elphinstone, Stirlingshire.

Around this time, tea overtakes ale as morning beverage.

1721

Robert Wodrow publishes *Sufferings of the Church of Scotland*.

1722

The Signet Library established in Edinburgh, as a professional resource for Writers to the Signet.

The pheasant is introduced to Scotland.

1723

History of My Own Times by Gilbert Burnet (1643–1715) published.

Society for the Improvement in the Knowledge of Agriculture founded in Edinburgh.

1724

'Levellers' among the Galloway peasantry attack enclosed land.

1725

Shawfield Riots caused by the Malt Tax.

A new Disarming Act passed.

General Wade commissions the Black Watch (42nd Regiment) to police the Highlands (12 May). Between now and 1736, General Wade constructs military roads in the Highlands.

A six-horse chaise seen in Inverness for the first time.

Allan Ramsay publishes *The Gentle Shepherd*.

Dumfries town council puts an under-master in charge of cock-fighting at the school. Scholars may bring a cock to fight on appointed days, for a fee of 12p Scots.

1727

Death of George I. Accession of George II.

Establishment of Commissioners and Trustees for Improving Manufactures and Fisheries.

Founding of Royal Bank of Scotland, first bank to employ the overdraft method.

1728

Iron smelting begins at Invergarry.

Inverness–Fort William road completed through the Great Glen.

Last burning of a witch, at Dornoch.

First larches planted in Scotland, at Dunkeld.

1728

Allan Ramsay opens the first circulating library in Scotland.

James Gibbs (1682–1754) publishes his *Book of Architecture*.

Two million yards of linen are produced.

1729

Foundation of Society of St Luke in Edinburgh, Scotland's first art institution.

Edinburgh Royal Infirmary established.

William Mackintosh of Borlum, imprisoned Jacobite commander, publishes *Essays in Ways and Means of Inclosing, Fallowing, Planting, Etc.*

1730

Francis Hutcheson appointed Professor of Moral Philosophy at Glasgow: first to abandon lectures in Latin.

Complete publication of *The Seasons* by James Thomson (1700–48).

Iron smelting at Abernethy, Speyside, using Tomintoul ore.

Perth–Dunkeld–Inverness road completed.

Edinburgh Royal Infirmary opened.

The cedar of Lebanon tree is introduced to Scotland.

1731

The Poor Man's Physician published in Edinburgh.

1732

William Adam begins the new Haddo House.

1733

The Original Secession from the Church of Scotland, led by Ebenezer Erskine.

1734

John Cockburn establishes the first planned village at Ormiston.

Sir Archibald Grant begins agricultural improvements at Monymusk.

Death of Rob Roy MacGregor (born 1671).

Robert Keith publishes *History of the Affairs of Church and State in Scotland.*

First recorded reference to the sword dance, or *gille calum.*

1735

Kelp manufacture begins on North Uist.

Mrs Henry Fletcher commences Holland linen manufacture. Glasgow has 47 ships engaged in the Atlantic trade.

1736

The Porteous Riot in Edinburgh.

Repeal of the Witchcraft Act of 1563.

First purpose-built theatre in Edinburgh.

Dr John Armstrong publishes *The Oeconomy of Love*, a sex manual for newlyweds, in verse.

1737

By now, simple inns are established at intervals along the new military roads.

1738

Allan Ramsay the Younger (1713–84), portrait painter, removes to London.

1739

Formation of the Black Watch as a regiment.

Publication of David Hume's *Treatise of Human Nature* and James Anderson's *Diplomata.*

Scots Magazine founded. Philosophical Society of Edinburgh founded by Thomas Ruddiman, later the Royal Society of Edinburgh.

1740

Around this time, cultivation of the turnip is introduced, and potatoes begin to become a staple rather than a luxury crop.

1740

Tobias Smollett (1721–71), author, moves to London.

Lord Lovat makes the first journey by coach from Inverness to Edinburgh.

Aberdeen Royal Infirmary founded.

Failure of crops throughout the country with subsequent hardship. Boys and youths kidnapped for sale to America.

The River Tay is frozen for six weeks from 1 January.

1741

First Gaelic–English dictionary by Alisdair MacMaighstir Alasdair, is published.

The miners' library at Leadhills is founded.

Granite starts to be used for buildings in Aberdeen.

Press-gang activity of the Royal Navy snatches away many fishermen and seamen.

1742

Edinburgh Ice Skating Club established.

1743

Last wolf killed, either by Cameron of Lochiel in Inverness-shire or by Eoghan MacQueen in Perthshire.

1744

Failure of French invasion plan.

Original Seceders split into 'Burghers' and 'Anti-Burghers'.

Honourable Company of Edinburgh Golfers established.

1745

Prince Charles Edward Stewart lands, first on Eriskay, then at Arisaig, and raises Cameron support (August). Muster of Jacobites at Glenfinnan (19 August).

Capture of Edinburgh (17 September).

Defeat of government army at Prestonpans (21 September).

Invasion of, and retreat from, England.

Tennant's Brewery set up in Glasgow.

Edinburgh's first wallpaper merchant opens for business.

Cattle plague breaks out in England, pushing up prices of Scottish cattle.

1746

Jacobite victory at Falkirk (17 January).

Jacobite defeat at Battle of Culloden (16 April).

Prince Charles Edward Stewart in hiding, then rescued by a French ship (September).

Highland dress and the bagpipe are officially proscribed.

Loch Arkaig treasure of 40,000 louis landed from France (May), its fate uncertain.

British Linen Company receives its charter.

Forest fire in Duach Valley, Moray, destroys 2.5 million trees.

1747

Aberdeen Journal founded.

1748

Act for the Abolition of Heritable Jurisdictions heralds final collapse of clan system.

Petition for 'Augmenting the Salaries and Other Incomes of the Schoolmasters of Scotland'.

Tobias Smollett publishes *The Adventures of Roderick Random.*

1749

Aberdeen Banking Company founded: first outside Edinburgh. Younger's Brewery set up at Holyrood, Edinburgh.

First stage-coach service from Glasgow to Edinburgh.

First Scottish chemical works, a vitriol factory at Prestonpans.

1750

Around this time, the Norn language of Shetland finally becomes obsolete.

Iron smelting using charcoal established in the Highlands at Bonawe.

New shops in Glasgow include a silversmith's and a haberdasher's.

It begins to be unusual for a farmer and his family to share all meals with the farm workers.

Around this time, the capercaillie becomes extinct.

1751

Alisdair MacMaighstir Alasdair publishes the first collection of original Gaelic poetry, *Ais-eiridh na Sean Chanain Albannaich* ('The Resurrection of the Old Scottish Language').

New Turnpike Road Act sets road improvement in motion.

Towns with more than 10,000 people are Edinburgh plus Leith (57,000), Glasgow (32,000), Aberdeen (15,500), Dundee (12,400). Only four other burghs exceed 5,000.

1752

Calendar reformed; eleven days removed to bring Scotland and England into line with Europe.

The 'Old New Year' continues to be celebrated in many places.

The Appin Murder: Colin Campbell of Glenure ('The Red Fox') killed, 14 May. James Stewart ('James of the Glens') tried and hanged for the crime.

1753

Slight shocks from the great Lisbon earthquake are felt throughout the country (1 November).

1754

James Justice publishes *The Scots Gardener's Director*.

Society of Golfers formed at St Andrews.

Allan Ramsay, the painter, returns to Edinburgh.

1755

Society for Encouraging Art, Science and Industry formed in Edinburgh.

Journeymen Woolcombers Society begun in Aberdeen.

Alexander Webster publishes *An Account of the Number of People in Scotland*, estimating the population at 1,265,380, of whom 51 per cent live north of the River Tay. Perthshire is the most populous county (120,116), followed by Aberdeen (116,168), then Midlothian (90,412).

1756

Death of William McGibbon, Scotland's leading eighteenth-century composer.

Around now, inoculation against smallpox is becoming increasingly common.

Between now and 1761, Joseph Black (1728–99) develops the theory of latent heat.

Duke of Argyll has 29,657 trees planted at Inveraray, including many foreign species.

1757

Greenock becomes a burgh (of barony).

James Watt (1736–1819) appointed mathematical instrument-maker to Glasgow University.

1759

Birth of Robert Burns (25 January).

William Robertson publishes his *History of Scotland* (from 1542 to 1603).

Foundation of the Carron Iron Company, largest in Europe.

1760

Death of George II. Accession of George III.

James Macpherson (1736–96) begins publication of his Ossian poems.

Thomas Braidwood (1750–98) opens Britain's first school for the deaf and dumb.

Edinburgh School of Design established.

Banks begin to be established in country towns.

Carpet weaving begins in Hawick and Kilmarnock. Coke smelting of iron begins.

1762

Around now, the fashionable dinner hour is advanced to three, or even four, o'clock.

1762

Completion of the Royal Exchange, Edinburgh.

1762

St Cecilia's Hall built in Edinburgh: first purpose-built concert hall.

1763

A windmill is erected at Stromness, Orkney, for milling grain.

1764

Joseph Black demonstrates that a balloon filled with hydrogen will rise.

1765

Alison Cockburn (1713–94), Scottish poet, publishes her version of 'The Flowers of the Forest'.

Society for the Importation of Forest Seeds established in Edinburgh by Dr John Hops, Professor of Botany.

By this time, wooden-tracked waggon-ways are in common use in the Fife collieries, using horse-power.

1767

Work begins on the New Town of Edinburgh, to the design of James Craig.

James Small patents the chain plough – use of it spreads rapidly.

1768

William Smellie launches the *Encyclopaedia Britannica* in Edinburgh.

Gaelic poems of Duncan Bàn MacIntyre (1724–1812) published.

Famine in the Western Isles and West Highlands, and again in 1769.

1769

Fenwick weavers form the first Co-operative Society (9 November).

James Watt (1736–1819) patents a separate steam condenser.

1770

William Hunter (1718–83), anatomist, establishes his 'Hunterian Museum' in London; to be bequeathed to Glasgow University.

Death of the Gaelic poet Alisdair MacMaighstir Alasdair (born c.1695).

Town of Ballater founded, around mineral wells.

The Crieff Cattle Tryst in disuse.

Act passed to establish Clyde Trust, to deepen and maintain the river below Glasgow.

Thirteen million yards of linen are produced.

John Broadwood (1732–1812) founds his piano manufactory in London.

James Bruce discovers the source of the Blue Nile.

By now potatoes are the main item of diet in the Highlands and Islands.

1771

Tobias Smollett publishes *The Expedition of Humphrey Clinker*. Henry Mackenzie publishes *The Man of Feeling*.

Value of tobacco imports peaks at around £490,000, three times the value in 1755. Re-exported tobacco accounts for 51 per cent of Scottish export value.

1772

Gavin Hamilton paints an Ossian cycle in Penicuik House.

Collapse of the Ayr bank of Douglas Heron.

Calico manufacture begins in Lanarkshire.

Smeaton builds a new bridge over the River Tay at Perth.

North Bridge of Edinburgh completed.

James Riggs sets up his Spade-making Works at Sanquhar.

1773

Robert Fergusson (1750–74) composes his poem, 'Auld Reekie'.

Building of Culzean Castle by James Adam (finished 1790).

John Erskine of Carnock (1695–1768) publishes his *Institutes of the Law of Scotland*.

Edinburgh Medical Journal established.

Dr Samuel Johnson and James Boswell tour the Highlands and Islands.

James Watt removes to England to pursue development of his improved steam engines.

James Gibbs (born 1682), architect of nave of St Nicholas, Aberdeen, and numerous London churches, dies.

1774

Register House, Edinburgh, built by Robert Adam.

1775

Partial emancipation of coal miners and salt-pan workers from serf-like status.

Iron smelting established at Furnace, Argyll, up to 1813.

1776

American War of Independence has a disastrous impact on Glasgow's tobacco trade.

Gaelic poems of Mary MacLeod (*c.*1615–*c.*1707) first published. Adam Smith (1723–90) publishes *The Wealth of Nations*. Lord Kames publishes *The Gentleman Farmer*.

Royal Observatory founded on Calton Hill, Edinburgh.

1777

Thirlage to local mills is ended, although money payments have to be made to compensate for multures.

The Highland Light Infantry formed.

Weatherby's Racing Calendar records a 5-day race meeting at Ayr.

1778

Atholl Highlanders, raised by Duke of Atholl, still in existence as a 'private army'.

Seaforth Highlanders raised by Earl of Seaforth.
Death of the Gaelic poet, Rob Donn MacKay (born 1714).
Edinburgh is estimated to have 400 illicit whisky stills.

1779
First large water-powered spinning mill is opened at Rothesay.
A large iron works is established at Wilsontown.

1780
Value of linen manufacturing has increased almost six-fold
  since 1730.

1781
Private whisky distilling (not for resale) is made illegal.
  Existence of around 1,000 small distilleries is estimated.
The Mound, Edinburgh begins to be built up, continuing to
  1820.
First Highland Games are held, at the Falkirk Cattle Tryst.

1782
Highland dress again allowed.
First umbrella seen in use in Edinburgh.
Bad harvest causes famine and deaths in the Highlands. Grain
  shortage results in efforts to ban whisky distilling.

1783
Beginning of the rule of Henry 'The Ninth' Dundas as political
  supremo of Scotland.
Royal Society of Edinburgh founded from the Philosophical
  Society.
Glasgow Advertiser (later *Glasgow Herald* then *The Herald*)
  founded. Glasgow Chamber of Commerce established.

1784
Forfeited estates of Jacobites restored.
Death of Allan Ramsay, portrait painter (born 1713).
Elspeth Buchan (1738–91) proclaims herself the Woman of
  Revelation.

1785

Founding of the Royal Highland and Agricultural Society.

J. Tytler makes the first hot air balloon ascent in Scotland, from Comely Bank to Restalrig, Edinburgh.

1785

By now, soft fruit bushes can be found in cottage and house gardens.

The Ayrshire breed of cow, and the Dunlop cheese, are both in active development at this time.

James Hutton (1726–97), pioneer geologist, expounds his *Theory of the Earth* to Royal Society of Edinburgh.

Signor Lunardi, the Italian balloonist, makes flights from Glasgow and Edinburgh, including one over the Firth of Forth.

1786

Robert Burns publishes the Kilmarnock edition of his poems.

John Anderson (1726–96) publishes *Institutes of Physics*.

Northern Lighthouse Board is set up.

Stage coaches introduced between Edinburgh and London.

David Dale (1739–1806) institutes cotton mills at New Lanark, using water-power from the River Clyde.

1787

Andrew Meikle (1719–1811) produces his threshing mill – the world's first fully successful thresher.

Kinnaird Head Lighthouse built.

New Club of Edinburgh founded as a dining club.

1788

Prince Charles Edward Stewart dies in Rome.

Alexander Nasmyth (1758–1840) paints Burns's portrait.

William Symington (1763–1831) launches a paddle steamer on Dalswinton Loch.

British Fisheries Society establishes port at Ullapool.

Direct Glasgow–London stage-coach service begins.

The Northern Meeting is established at Inverness (June 11).

1789

William Cullen publishes *Treatise on Materia Medica*.
The Old Quad, Edinburgh University, built by Robert Adam.

1790

Bernera Barracks, Glenelg, abandoned.
First publication of pibroch music.
James Bruce of Kinnaird (1730–94) publishes *Travels to Discover the Source of the Nile*.
Opening of the Forth and Clyde Canal.
By now the Clydesdale horse breed is established.
Duke of Atholl establishes the first deer forest.

1791

Publication of the *Statistical Account of Scotland* begins, until 1799.

1792

Association of Friends of the People for Parliamentary Reform started by Thomas Muir and William Skirving. They hold three conventions this year and next.
Opening of the Monkland Canal.
Sir Alexander Mackenzie (1764–1820) is first European to cross the Rocky Mountains.
James Adam (1730–94) designs the Glasgow Infirmary.
Robert Adam (born 1728), architect of Register House, Edinburgh, and many other buildings, dies.
William Murdoch develops gas lighting.

1793

War with France begins. Political trials of suspect 'radicals' this year and next.
Thomas Muir sentenced to 14 years' transportation for sedition.
Cameron Highlanders regiment raised by Cameron of Lochiel.
Work begins on the Crinan Canal.

1794

Duke of Argyll raises the Argyll Highlanders; Duke of Gordon raises the Gordon Highlanders.

Board of Agriculture publishes *The General View of Agriculture* to encourage progressive techniques.

1795

Aberdeen obtains a Police Act for civic order, street paving, and so on.

Opening of Glasgow Royal Infirmary.

The Black Watch are granted the right to wear the 'red hackle' on the left side of their bonnets.

Regular race meetings are established around now in Ayr, Edinburgh, Dumfries, Kelso, Hamilton, and other places.

1796

Opening of the Andersonian Institution, Glasgow, later Royal Technical College, ultimately University of Strathclyde.

Work begins on Aberdeenshire Canal, later converted to railway track.

Death of Robert Burns (21 July).

1797

Militia Act. Riots in Tranent against conscription.

George Mealmaker, radical weaver of Dundee, transported for sedition.

Edinburgh opens its first Magdalene Asylum, for the reformation of 'fallen women'.

1798

Ayrshire Yeomanry raised by Earl of Cassilis.

Opening of Dundee Infirmary.

St Rollox Chemical Works established in Glasgow.

1799

Napoleonic Wars begin.

Liberation of the coal miners from partial serfdom.

East Docks at Leith are built.

Mungo Park (1771–1806) publishes *Travels in the Interior of Africa*. Robert Burns's *Love and Liberty* poems published as *The Jolly Beggars*.

Sir Henry Raeburn (1756–1823) paints a famous portrait of the violinist Neil Gow, among many other cultural and social figures.

1800

Ayrshire is first county to establish a rural police force.

Aberdeen New Streets Act passed: building of Union Street commenced.

1801

First official census shows population as 1,608,000.

The world's first paddle steamer, *Charlotte Dundas*, used as a tug.

Robert Brown (1773–1858), botanist, sails with Matthew Flinders to survey Australia.

1802

Sir Walter Scott publishes *Minstrelsy of the Scottish Border*.

Foundation of the *Edinburgh Review*.

1803

Highland Roads and Bridges Commission established. Thomas Telford begins road construction.

First all-iron swing plough developed by Gray of Uddingston.

1804

Construction of Caledonian Canal begins.

1805

Building of the Hunterian Museum, Glasgow.

Sir David Wilkie (1785–1841), artist, leaves Edinburgh for London.

Sir Walter Scott publishes *The Lay of the Last Minstrel*.

Weaving of Paisley pattern shawls begins around now in Paisley.

1806

Royal Highland and Agricultural Society offers a prize for a practicable mechanical reaper.

1806

Glasgow, Paisley and Johnstone Canal begun.

1807

Construction of the Bell Rock lighthouse, completed 1811, by Robert Stevenson.

Death of Neil Gow, celebrated fiddler and composer of strathspeys (born 1727).

Measles epidemic causes many deaths.

1808

The Court of Session is reorganized into two divisions under the Lord President and the Lord Justice Clerk.

Jamieson's *Etymological Dictionary of the Scottish Language* published.

Hugh Watson, pioneer of Aberdeen-Angus cattle breeding, starts his farm.

1809

Completion of the first complete topographical survey of Scotland.

Death of Sir John Moore at Corunna (born Glasgow 1761).

Caledonian Horticultural Society established.

The bothy system is coming into use in larger farms in Angus and the northeast.

Lachlan MacQuarie appointed governor of New South Wales.

1810

Surveys confirm Ben Nevis as highest mountain; previously thought to be Ben Macdhui.

Walter Scott publishes *The Lady of the Lake*.

World's first savings bank established, the Parish Bank Friendly Society of Ruthwell, by the Reverend Henry Duncan (20 June).

Lead mining still carried on; yield is 1,400 tons.

John Loudon McAdam (1756–1836) begins road construction.

Commercial Bank of Scotland founded (24 March).

Hunters for cairngorm stones haunt the Cairngorm Mountains.

1811

Census shows population as 1,806,000.

Crofting system begins to oust runrig in the Highlands and Islands.

Death of David Ritchie, 'the Black Dwarf', 3 feet 6 inches tall, born 1735 near Peebles.

1812

American War does severe damage to cotton trade, up to 1814.

Henry Bell (1767–1830) builds steamship *Comet,* pioneer of practical steam navigation.

Lanarkshire weavers jailed for 'combining' in a trade union.

Strawberries grown commercially at Roslin.

1813

Dissatisfaction and unrest among workers in the post-war slump, especially handloom weavers. Court of Session fixes their pay but employers ignore this.

1814

Strathnaver Clearances in Sutherland.

Anonymous publication of Walter Scott's first novel, *Waverley.*

Last sea-witch in Orkney sells winds to sailors.

Earl of Buchan sets up a colossal Wallace statue, near Dryburgh.

Heavy storms, with numerous shipwrecks (16–17 December).

1815

The Corn Laws push up food prices, creating hunger among the unemployed, and further unrest.

Establishment of trial by jury in civil cases.

1816

Sir Walter Scott begins building of Abbotsford.

David Brewster (1781–1868) invents the kaleidoscope.

Small Stills Act helps reduce illegal whisky distilling.

1817

Treason trials of radical agitators.

Tax of 4d put on newspapers and magazines.

Edinburgh's first Police Act.

Founding of *The Scotsman* newspaper and *Blackwood's Magazine*.

First Scottish steam railway (goods) between Kilmarnock and Troon.

Denny's Shipyard opens at Dumbarton.

Union Canal, from Edinburgh to Glasgow, begun.

First Braemar Highland Gathering.

1818

Walter Scott publishes *Rob Roy* and *Heart of Midlothian*.

Measles, typhus and whooping cough epidemics.

First iron passenger ship launched on the River Clyde.

Colonel 145, first in the Aberdeen-Angus herd book, is born.

1820

Government arrests 20 members of Glasgow Radical Committee.

Skirmish of Bonnymuir between Radical marchers and Kilsyth Yeomanry (5 April): 50 men tried for treason, 3 hanged, 19 transported.

Walter Scott is made a baronet.

About now, 'tweed' becomes a popular fabric in Glasgow and London.

The Edinburgh Botanic Garden resited at Inverleith.

1821

Census shows population as 2,092,000.

Edinburgh School of Arts established, later the Watt Institution, ultimately Heriot-Watt University.

John Galt (1779–1839) publishes *Annals of the Parish*. Lady Nairne (1766–1845) publishes her songs pseudonymously in *The Scottish Minstrel*.

1822

King George IV visits Edinburgh, the first monarch to do so since Charles II.

Licence fee on whisky distilling reduced to £10; duty reduced: smuggling dies away, development of the whisky industry begins.

Jute first imported to Dundee.

The kelp industry of the west collapses.

Opening of the Caledonian Canal (November).

First Highland Agricultural Show.

John Dubh MacCrimmon, last of the celebrated piping family, dies.

1823

Foundation of the Bannatyne Club, for the publication of old texts.

Sir Henry Raeburn (1756–1823) is appointed King's Limner and Painter in Scotland.

Dick Veterinary College founded, Edinburgh.

White Star Shipping Line founded in Aberdeen.

Lifting of import duties on salt (January) has a severe effect on Scottish salt industry.

Charles Macintosh (1776–1843) patents his 'proof cloth': his invention of rubberized waterproofing leads to the 'Macintosh' coat.

Hugh Clapperton (1788–1827) crosses the Sahara Desert.

1824

James Hogg (1770–1835) publishes *The Private Memoirs and Confessions of a Justified Sinner*.

Sir Walter Scott publishes *Redgauntlet*.

Edinburgh sets up the first municipal fire brigade.

1825

William Burn (1789–1870) designs Edinburgh Academy.

National Napoleonic Wars Memorial on Calton Hill, Edinburgh, is begun by W.H. Playfair but never completed.

Ayrshire Colliers' Union established.

1825

The cotton industry is estimated to employ 151,000 people.

Abolition of salt duty ruins the Scots salt-pan industry.

Edinburgh Royal High School built by Thomas Hamilton (1784–1858).

James Chalmers (1782–1853) invents adhesive postage stamps.

David Douglas (1798–1834) discovers the giant fir in North America.

1826

Royal Scottish Academy founded.

First Scottish public railway, between Monkland and Kirkintilloch (steam and horse).

Incorporation of Edinburgh–Dalkeith Railway (horse traction) and Dundee and Newtyle Railway (horse and cable).

First Scottish tile-works, at Cessnock.

Dr Robert Knox (1791–1862) opens his anatomy school in Edinburgh.

Glasgow City Mission founded.

1827

The High Court sentences its youngest criminal, a nine-year-old boy, to 18 months for theft.

Captain James Stirling founds Perth, Australia.

Patrick Bell (1799–1869) invents the first effective reaping machine.

Robert Wilson invents the screw propellor.

1828

Population of the island of Rum is cleared out to America.

Home Drummond Act begins licensing of public houses. Pubs must close for the hour of divine service.

Publication of Rob Donn Mackay's (1714–78) Gaelic poems.

J B Neilson (1792–1865) invents hot-blast iron-refining.

Building of the lighthouse at Cape Wrath.

1829

Trial of Burke and Hare for body-snatching in Edinburgh; Burke hanged; Hare turns King's Evidence.

Building of the Royal Exchange, Glasgow.

Catholic Emancipation Act passed.

Restoration of High Kirk of St Giles in Edinburgh.

Damaging floods in Moray

1830

Death of George IV. Accession of William (III of Scotland, IV of England). Whigs come to power in Westminster Parliament.

Sir Charles Lyell (1797–1875) publishes *Principles of Geology*, completed 1833.

Aeneas Coffey's patent still gives boost to whisky-making.

First iron steamship, *Lord Dundas*, built on the River Clyde.

David Hutcheson organizes steamer services from the Clyde to Argyll.

From around now, Shetland ponies are extensively used in coal mining.

1831

Census shows population as 2,364,000.

Norse chessmen dating from *c.*1200 found on Lewis.

Sir James Ross (1800–62) locates the Magnetic North Pole.

Scotland's first effective steam railway, Glasgow to Garnkirk, is opened.

James Smith publishes *Remarks on Thorough Drainage and Deep Ploughing*.

Berwickshire Naturalists' Club founded.

Cholera strikes for the first time, with deaths estimated at 10,000.

1832

Reform Act passed: 40,000 march in celebration in Edinburgh.

1833

Scottish MPs increased from 45 to 53.

Franchise extended to 60,000 men (householders of £10 in the burghs and proprietors of £10 or tenants of £50 rental in the country districts).

Dundee and Newtyle Railway completed. Dean Bridge built over the Water of Leith in Edinburgh.

Death of Sir Walter Scott.

Continuing outbreaks of cholera cause at least 10,000 deaths.

1833

Slavery abolished in British dominions.

Burgh Reform Act extends electoral rights in burgh elections to all rate-payers.

Abbotsford Club founded to publish historical source material. Thomas Carlyle publishes *Sartor Resartus*.

1834

General Assembly passes Veto Act, empowering congregations to reject the choice of a patron. House of Lords rejects this.

Countess of Dunmore organizes first sales of Harris tweed in London.

Thomas Carlyle moves to London from Scotland.

Thomas Henderson (1798–1844) becomes first Astronomer Royal for Scotland.

Society of Golfers becomes the Royal and Ancient Golf Club. First Scottish cricket championship, between Perth and Glasgow Cricket Clubs.

1835

Dalkeith Scientific Association is formed.

A cock pit is erected in Hope Street, Glasgow, with much gambling activity.

1836

First iron ship is built on the River Tay, at Perth.

Three-month strike of cotton workers.

North of Scotland Bank founded, Aberdeen.

Serious typhus epidemic in Glasgow and other urban areas, with many deaths.

First Champion Clydesdale Horse competition.

First ascent of Sgurr nan Gillean on Skye, by Principal James Forbes of St Andrews University.

1837

Death of William IV. Accession of Victoria.

J G Lockhart publishes *Memoirs of the Life of Sir Walter Scott*, completed 1838.

Thomas Carlyle publishes *The French Revolution*.

James Forbes (1809–68) discovers the polarisation of heat.

The capercaillie is re-introduced from Sweden.

1838

Chartism becomes a force for political reform.

Five leaders of the 1836 cotton strike sentenced to transportation (given a free pardon in 1840).

Clydesdale Bank founded in Glasgow. Caledonian Bank founded in Inverness.

Royal Caledonian Curling Club founded.

1839

By now, over 80 local Chartist Associations have been formed.

James Nasmyth (1808–90) develops the steam hammer.

First Aberdeen clipper, *Scottish Maid*, launched.

Sir James Ross begins Antarctic exploration.

Spalding Club is founded in Aberdeen to print historical material relating to the North East.

1840

Kirkpatrick Macmillan makes the first true bicycle.

Glasgow School of Art and Architectural Institute of Scotland founded.

Great auk ceases to breed in the Hebrides.

1841

Census shows population as 2,620,000. Sixteen per cent of Glasgow's population is Irish-born (44,000 out of 270,000).

Sheriff Watson establishes 'ragged schools' in Aberdeen.

Thomas Carlyle (1795–1881) publishes *On Heroes and Hero-Worship*. Hugh Miller (1802–56) publishes *The Old Red Sandstone*. Sir Thomas Dick Lauder (1784–1848) publishes *Legends and Tales of the Highlands*.

Robert Napier starts first yard for all-iron ships at Govan and builds first iron warship for the Royal Navy, HMS *Jackal*.

'Tennant's Stalk', 455-foot smoke-stack, built at St Rollox Chemical Works, Glasgow.

1842

Chadwick Report condemns Glasgow as most insanitary town in Britain.

Year of commercial disasters in which numerous banks fail.

Scottish Patriotic Society founded to encourage emigration.

James Forbes invents the seismometer.

Edinburgh and Glasgow are joined by railway.

Donaldson's Hospital, Edinburgh, built by W H Playfair (1789–1857).

1843

Employment of women in the mines ceases.

Disruption of Church of Scotland – establishment of Free Church. Around 500 churches are built in the year following.

First performance of *The Messiah* in Glasgow.

Robert Adamson, photography pioneer, develops calotype process.

James Braid writes first medical paper on hypnosis.

1844

Incorporation of the North British Railway Company; its first line from Edinburgh to Berwick.

Skerryvore lighthouse constructed.

1845

Board of Supervision of Commissioners for Poor Relief established.

Poor Law Act extends residence requirement for someone to be eligible for poor relief from three to five years.

Efforts to stop the 'bondager' system of unpaid female labour in Lothian fail.

Electric telegraph begins operation.

Incorporation of the Caledonian Railway Company, between Glasgow and Carlisle (opened September 1847).

Robert William Thompson (1822–73) patents a pneumatic tyre.

Completion of the Scott Monument in Princes Street, Edinburgh.

1846

Burgh Reform Act removes old trading monopolies of burghs and guilds.

Corn Laws repealed.

Serious typhus epidemic sweeps through Glasgow, with many deaths.

The Famine Relief Committee finds that potatoes represent up to 88 per cent of the diet in the Highlands, and 25 per cent in the Lowlands.

Public Money Drainage Act makes £2,000,000 available for land drainage loans.

1847

Failure of the potato crop causes famine in the Highlands and Islands between now and 1850.

Thomas Guthrie (1803–73) publishes *Plea for Ragged Schools*.

United Presbyterian Church founded.

Educational Institute of Scotland founded.

Sir James Young Simpson (1811–70) originates use of ether at childbirth.

1848

James 'Paraffin' Young (1811–83) establishes the paraffin oil industry from shale deposits. Michael Nairn begins making linoleum at Kirkcaldy.

1848

Ten thousand Chartists demonstrate on Calton Hill, Edinburgh; Chartist riots in Glasgow (March).

Pure jute cloth first produced in Dundee.

Leather golf balls replaced by gutta-percha.

Representatives of 200 bowling clubs meet in Glasgow to agree a standard set of rules.

Outbreaks of cholera throughout the country this year and next.

1849

Seventy people crushed to death in false fire alarm in a Glasgow theatre.

David Livingstone (1813–73) begins missionary activity in Central Africa.

Private Money Drainage Act stimulates founding of companies to finance drainage and land improvement.

World's first train ferry built by Napier at Govan, the *Leviathan*.

1850

Lothian shale oil industry begins.

Completion of the Glasgow and South-Western Railway, Glasgow to Dumfries (October).

Introduction of the world's first train ferry service across the Firth of Forth, from Granton to Burntisland, by North British Railway.

Scotland has 21 poorhouses.

By now, runrig cultivation has almost vanished in the Highlands.

1851

Emigration Society founded on Skye.

Completion of Donaldson's Hospital, Edinburgh.

Glasgow Natural History Society founded.

David Hutcheson & Company establish steamer routes in Western Isles.

Alexander Bain develops an electric clock.

1852

Highland Emigration Society formed.

An amateur dramatic society is formed in Falkirk.

Triangulation Survey of Great Britain is completed; surveyors celebrate in the open air with a giant pudding.

1853

Formation of the National Association for the Vindication of Scottish Rights.

Public drinking of alcohol is restricted to licensed premises. Sunday closing of pubs is introduced.

Opening of the Deeside Railway.

Purchase and rebuilding of Balmoral Castle by Albert, Prince Consort.

John Ruskin's *Edinburgh Lectures* popularize the Gothic style.

Founding of Allan Glen's School, Glasgow and completion of Daniel Stewart's College, Edinburgh.

The Royal National Lifeboat Institution has 7 stations in Scotland.

A 28-gram nugget of gold is found at Kildonan, Sutherland.

1854

Crimean War begins – Scottish regiments sent out. The 93rd Highlanders hold the 'thin red line' at Balaclava.

Opening of the Great North of Scotland Railway between Aberdeen and Huntly (September 19).

Hugh Miller publishes *My Schools and Schoolmasters*.

Outbreaks of cholera throughout the country.

1855

United Coal and Iron Miners' Association of Scotland founded.

Methylated Spirits Act passed to restrict human consumption.

Eighty-nine per cent of men can sign their names on marriage certificates; seventy-seven per cent of women.

Glasgow begins to build the pipeline for the supply of pure water from Loch Katrine.

Introduction of the first railway in the Highlands, Inverness to Nairn.

David Livingstone discovers the Victoria Falls.

1856

Henry Cockburn's (1779–1854) *Memorials of His Time* published.

Eliza Edmonston's *Sketches and Tales of the Shetland Islands* first popularizes Fair Isle knitting.

1857

Indian Mutiny breaks out. Scottish regiments in action, including the relief of Lucknow.

Board of Commissioners in Lunacy established.

First steel steamship constructed on the Clyde.

Crash of the Western Bank.

Madeleine Smith tried in Glasgow for murder of her lover, verdict not proven (September).

David Livingstone publishes *Missionary Travels in South Africa*. Donald MacLeod publishes *Gloomy Memories of the Highlands of Scotland*, first in Canada.

1858

Honours degree courses instituted at Scottish Universities. The position of Rector as students' elected representative is established.

Free Church builds the Assembly Hall on the Mound, Edinburgh.

George MacDonald (1824–1905) publishes *Phantastes*. R M Ballantine publishes *The Coral Island*.

Edinburgh Academicals Football Club formed (to play rugby).

1859

Large numbers of men (five per cent of eligible population) join the Volunteer Movement, sparked by French invasion fears.

Loch Katrine water is piped to Glasgow. Queen Victoria opens the scheme (15 October).

Scottish National Gallery opens (21 March).

Samuel Smiles (1813–94) publishes *Self-Help*.

1860

Union of King's and Marischal Colleges as Aberdeen University.

The Book of Deer (11th/12th century Gospels with Gaelic marginal notes) is found in Cambridge University Library.

J F Campbell (1822–85) begins to publish *Popular Tales of the West Highlands*.

Glasgow Choral Union holds its first music festival.

The Scotsman reports that in Europe only Austria has a higher illegitimacy rate than Scotland.

Portable steam sawmills now in use in lumber industry.

Golf Open Championship introduced.

1861

Census establishes Scotland as having 787 islands, of which 602 are uninhabited.

American Civil War creates huge growth in Dundee jute industry and hits the cotton industry.

Founding of the Royal Scottish Museum in Edinburgh.

Tom Morris (1821–1908) becomes golf professional at St Andrews; wins British Championship Belt four times.

Queen's Park Football Club formed (9 June).

John McDouall Stuart is first man to walk across Australia, north-to-south.

1862

Burgh Police Act, enabling local authorities to enforce building regulations. Salmon Fisheries Act.

1863

Osgood Mackenzie begins to establish the gardens at Inverewe.

1863

James Clerk Maxwell (1831–79) develops theory of magnetic waves.

1864

Last public execution in Edinburgh: George Bryce for the razor murder of a young woman.

Completion of railway from Perth to Inverness; incorporation of the Highland Railway Company.

James Augustus Grant (1827–92), explorer, publishes *A Walk Across Africa*.

1865

Last public execution in Glasgow: Dr E. Pritchard for murder of his wife and mother-in-law.

Sir Archibald Geikie (1835–1924), geologist, publishes *The Scenery of Scotland*.

Cattle rearing heavily hit by rinderpest from the Continent.

1866

Glasgow 'tickets' small houses to stipulate maximum number of dwellers.

Police Act to suppress brothels and street prostitution.

The fort at Fort William abandoned and largely demolished.

Church of Scotland permits use of organ music in churches.

Cholera outbreaks throughout the country.

Tom Morris (1821–1908) wins his fourth and last Open Golf Championship.

1867

Franchise extended to all adult males. Scottish Women's Suffrage Society formed, in Edinburgh.

Public Health Act for Scotland passed.

Singer Sewing Machine factory established near Dumbarton.

Building of the Albert Institute, Dundee.

1868

Scottish Reform Act passed (13 July). Franchise extended to all male householders.

Scotland's first Ladies' Educational Association formed, in Edinburgh, to promote higher education for women.

Scottish Co-operative Wholesale Society founded.

Queen Victoria publishes *Leaves from a Journal of Our Life in the Highlands*.

1869

Female householders are given right to vote in municipal elections.

Peak of pig-iron production, at 1,206,000 tons.

Sailing ship *Cutty Sark* launched at Dumbarton (22 November).

Ramblers About Glasgow Club formed.

1870

New Glasgow University buildings on Gilmorehill completed (November) except for the spire (1887).

Medical students riot in Edinburgh against women attending anatomy lectures.

Thomas Lipton (1850–1931) opens his first grocery shop in Glasgow.

The Kildonan gold-field in Sutherland is closed down by the landowners.

Powderhall racing track set up, in Edinburgh.

1871

Gaelic Society of Inverness founded.

Paisley Museum established.

Tramcars begin to run in Edinburgh.

North British Railway introduces the first 4–4–0 express locomotive.

Scotland win the first Rugby International against England.

1872

Voting in elections by secret ballot introduced.

1873

Dundee Museum and Art Gallery established.

Steel Company of Scotland founded.

Education Act ensures universal education from 5–13 years of age.

Scottish Education Department set up.

First international football match, Scotland v England, results in an 0–0 draw. Second Rugby International is won by England.

1873

James Clerk Maxwell publishes *Treatise on Electricity and Magnetism*.

Alfred Nobel establishes a dynamite factory at Ardeer.

Dundee has ten steam-powered whaling ships.

Death of David Livingstone at Ujiji, East Africa.

Sankey and Moody begin a ten-year religious revival campaign throughout the country.

Severe summer storms with several deaths (22–23 July).

Formation of the Scottish Football Association, with seven member clubs.

Scottish Football Union formed (3 March) for Rugby Football. Scottish Football Association Cup Competition set up, won by Queen's Park. Rugby International a draw with England. Founding of Glasgow Rangers F. C.

1874

Repeal of the Patronage Act 'relatying to the Church of Scotland'.

Wick and Thurso linked to Inverness by rail (July).

Caledon Shipyard founded in Dundee.

Building of the harbour at Buckie, until 1880.

SFA Cup won by Queen's Park. Rugby International won by England.

1875

Artisans' and Labourers' Dwellings Act passed.

Factories Act raises minimum age of child workers to ten years; ten-hour working day established.

Cockburn Association founded in Edinburgh (first civic society).

Episcopal Church founds an orphanage at Aberlour.

Eighteen Gypsy families found still living around Kirk Yetholm.

The 1745 Monument erected at Glenfinnan.

Institute of Scottish Bankers founded in Edinburgh: first professional banking body.

SFA Cup won by Queen's Park. Rugby International drawn with England.

1876

Residence requirement for someone to be eligible for poor relief is restored to three years.

Tramcars begin to run in Dundee.

W F Skene (1809–92) publishes *Celtic Scotland* between now and 1880.

The staff-head, or *coigreach*, of St Fillan is acquired by the Museum of Antiquities from its hereditary keeper, Alexander Dewar.

Alexander Bain (1818–1903) founds the journal *Mind*.

Alexander Graham Bell (1847–1922), inventor of the telephone, emigrates to the USA.

SFA Cup won by Queen's Park. Rugby International won by England.

1877

Several whisky companies amalgamate to form The Distillers' Company Ltd.

Galloway Cattle Society founded.

Clydesdale Horse Stud Book set up.

SFA Cup won by Vale of Leven. Scotland beat England in Rugby International.

1878

Crash of the City of Glasgow Bank.

Roman Catholic episcopal hierarchy re-established.

1879

Fine Art Institute Building, Glasgow, designed by John James Burnet.

First Tay Bridge opened (1 June).

Dollar Academy founded.

William MacGonagall (1830–1902) publishes his first collection of verse.

African Lakes Company founded in Glasgow 'to advance the Kingdom of God by honest trade'.

SFA Cup won by Vale of Leven. Rugby International drawn with England.

1879

Collapse of the first Tay Bridge (28 December), with the loss of some 90 passengers and train crew.

Sir James Murray (1837–1915) commences work on *The Oxford English Dictionary*.

Establishment of Edinburgh Dental Hospital.

Building of Central and St Enoch Stations, in Glasgow.

David Hutcheson & Company becomes David MacBrayne & Company, synonymous with Western Isles transport.

Formation of Aberdeen-Angus Cattle Society.

SFA Cup won by Vale of Leven. Rugby International drawn with England.

1880

Around now, week long summer holidays for workers become usual (normally unpaid).

First Ordnance Survey maps of Scotland published.

Society of Antiquaries founded (18 December).

Callander–Oban Railway completed (July).

SFA Cup won by Queen's Park. England win Rugby International.

1881

Census shows population at 3.7 million.

The 91st Argyllshire Highlanders and 93rd Sutherland Highlanders combined as the Argyll & Sutherland Highlanders.

Foundation of the Highland Reel and Strathspey Society.

First torchlight procession of Up Helly Aa in Lerwick, Shetland.

SFA Cup won by Queen's Park. Rugby International drawn with England.

1882

Formation of the Highland Land League.

'Battle of the Braes' in Skye between crofters and police (11 April).

R L Stevenson (1850–94) publishes *Treasure Island*.

The 'Glasgow Boys' group of artists flourishes between now and *c*.1895.

Academy of Music for Scotland established in Edinburgh (September).

Chair of Celtic Studies founded at Edinburgh University; Gaelic taught at university for the first time.

University College, Dundee, founded; later known as Queen's College.

Scottish Texts Society founded.

Slight earthquake felt over the whole country (2 February).

SFA Cup won by Queen's Park. Scotland beat England in Rugby International.

1883

The 'Crofters' War' continues: appointment of Royal Commission to review the situation.

Steamer *Daphne* capsizes at launch on the Clyde; 124 die.

Explosions at Glasgow Gasworks (January) and the Forth and Clyde Canal aqueduct at Keppoch Hill (February) are ascribed to Irish terrorist activity. 'Glasgow Dynamiters' sentenced to penal servitude.

Deer forests take up 1,709,892 acres.

Sir William Smith (1854–1914) establishes the Boys' Brigade.

First Carnegie Free Library opens in Dunfermline.

Alexander Mackenzie publishes *The Highland Clearances*.

SFA Cup won by Dumbarton. England win Rugby International.

1884

Third Reform Act extends voting rights to farm labourers, among all male occupiers.

Twelve additional Scottish MPs (total now 70) and constituencies are realigned.

Uig crofters band to resist eviction, on Skye. Government sends a gunboat and 250 marines.

W Y MacGregor paints *Vegetable Stall*, a fine painting in the new French style.

Miss Cranston's Tearooms open in Glasgow.

Royal Scottish Geographical Society founded. Observatory established on summit of Ben Nevis, until 1903.

Heavy thunderstorms cause death and destruction in Edinburgh (August).

A five–foot salmon, weighing 80 pounds, is netted in the Tay (December), believed to be the biggest ever.

SFA Cup won by Queen's Park. England win Rugby International.

1885

Re-establishment of post of Secretary of State for Scotland.

Five crofters from Valtos (Lewis) sentenced to short terms for defiance of writs from Court of Session.

Coatbridge is made a burgh.

Monday holidays become common, as a substitute for the no-longer-observed fast days.

Steel output reaches 241,000 tons.

Founding of the Federation of Burns Clubs.

Founding of Aberdeen Art Gallery.

J M Robertson publishes *The Perversion of Scotland*, critique of contemporary culture.

National Museum of Antiquities begun in Edinburgh (opened 1890).

Heavy snow in May causes the death of many cattle and sheep in the north-east.

A brilliant display of over 600 meteors occurs on 27 November.

Two remarkable results in the SFA Cup: Arbroath 36, Bon Accord 0; and Dundee Harp 35, Aberdeen Rovers 0. Cup won by Renton. No Rugby International.

1886

Crofters' (Holdings) Act passed. Crofters' Commission set up.

Scottish Home Rule Association formed.

Six Skye crofters sentenced to six months each for mobbing and rioting.

Glasgow's first underground (steam) railway opened.

Six people die in a 'novel accident' at Crarae granite quarry, choked to death by fumes.

Over 30,000 people celebrate centenary of Kilmarnock Edition of Burns, at Kilmarnock (August).

R L Stevenson publishes *Dr Jekyll and Mr Hyde* and *Kidnapped*.

Mrs E Mouat of Shetland is rescued off the Norwegian coast, only survivor from a small boat that drifted away accidentally (November).

Earthquakes shake Uist and Shetland (October).

SFA Cup won by Queen's Park. Rugby International drawn with England.

1887

Queen Victoria's Golden Jubilee celebrations include a dinner for 6,000 poor people in Glasgow.

Riots by Blantyre miners destroy shops and property; the military are called in (February).

Seventy die in pit explosion in Blantyre (28 May).

Squatters on Lewis invade deer forests, claiming the deer are ruining pasture land (November).

1888

Completion of the new Tay Bridge.

Unveiling of the Wallace statue at the national Wallace Monument, Stirling (25 June).

Sir David Bruce (1855–1931) identifies the *Brucella* bacterium.

Gaelic Society of Glasgow founded.

Glasgow Rangers FC moves from Kinning to Ibrox Park. Glasgow Celtic FC founded by Brother Wilfred.

SFA Cup won by Hibernian. Rugby International drawn with England. The Cairngorm Club founded.

1888

The 'Goschen Formula' assesses Scottish/English share of government expenditure as 11/80.

Dundee is made a city.

Formation of Scottish Labour Party.

First conference of the Home Rule Association.

Fire at Mauricewood Colliery, Midlothian: 70 miners die.

Reformatory ship *Cumberland*, in the Clyde, set on fire by inmates: 400 escape.

John Boyd Dunlop (1840–1921) develops the pneumatic tyre.

Higher and Lower Grade school leaving certificate introduced.

A plague of rats afflicts many parts of the Lowlands.

SFA Cup won by Renton. Renton defeat English cup-holders, West Bromwich Albion, on 19 May to become 'world champions'. No Rugby International.

1889

Institution of elected County Councils.

J M Barrie (1860–1937) publishes *A Window in Thrums*.

Opening of National Portrait Gallery, Edinburgh (15 July), and completion of Glasgow Municipal Building, George Square (7 October).

George Henry paints *Galloway Landscape*, fine Impressionist-style work.

Eight hundred Catholics make a pilgrimage to Iona in honour of St Columba.

First burning of a longship in the Up Helly Aa celebration, Lerwick, Shetland.

First milking machine patented by William Murchland of Kilmarnock.

Dairy School for Scotland established near Kilmarnock.

Earthquake damages houses in Inverness and Forres. A violent gale wrecks numerous vessels (16 November).

SFA Cup won by Third Lanark. No Rugby International. Scottish Mountaineering Club founded.

1890

Mr Gladstone addresses Midlothian electors at the Corn Exchange, Edinburgh, for two hours 'without apparent fatigue'.

Sir James Frazer (1854–1941) begins publication of *The Golden Bough*.

An arm bone, allegedly a relic of St Giles, is found in restoration of his High Kirk in Edinburgh.

Completion of the Forth Railway Bridge. Railway strike paralyses transport (December–January).

White-tailed sea eagle extinct in Scotland by this year.

Scottish Football League established, eleven members in the first season. Rangers and Dumbarton are joint champions. SFA Cup won by Queen's Park. England win Rugby International.

1891

Elementary school fees abolished.

James Keir Hardie elected as first Independent Labour member (for a London seat).

Founding of *An Comunn Gaidhealach*.

First National Mod held at Oban.

Motherwell station wrecked in riot during railwaymen's strike.

Sir Hugh Munro publishes his tables of mountains over 3,000 feet in the *Scottish Mountaineering Journal* (September), listing 283 summits.

1892

Professor Norman Collie, FRS, sees the Grey Man of Ben Macdhui.

Twentieth football international with England, at Blackburn. England win 2–1 (4 April). SFA Cup won by Heart of Midlothian. Scotland beat England in Rugby International.

1892

Scottish Secretary of State becomes a member of the Cabinet.

Commission on Deer Forests appointed.

Miners go on strike (March).

Scottish Universities allow women to become undergraduates.

Sir Patrick Geddes (1854–1932) establishes world's first 'sociological laboratory' in Edinburgh.

Glasgow's first women doctors employed at Samaritan Hospital.

H E Moss of Greenock builds the first of the 'Moss Empire' halls, in Edinburgh.

Last Gypsy king, Charles Faa-Blythe, crowned at Kirk Yetholm. By now only a handful of Gypsy families remain.

Widespread flu epidemic (January).

Plague of fieldmice reported in several country districts (April–June).

SFA Cup won by Celtic. England win Rugby International. Scottish Bowling Association founded in Glasgow (12 September).

1893

Lord Mayors of London and Dublin make a state visit to Edinburgh.

Last whaling trip is made from Peterhead, by the *Windward* (18 April).

Glasgow Art Gallery begun. Royal Observatory moves from Calton Hill to Blackford Hill, Edinburgh.

Professionalism finally accepted in football. Football League sets up a Second Division. SFA Cup won by Queen's Park, for the last time. Scotland beat England in Rugby International. Camanachd Association formed in Kingussie to regulate shinty.

1894

Local Government Board for Scotland takes over responsibility from Board of Commissioners for Poor Relief.

William Sharp (1855–1905) publishes – as Fiona MacLeod – *The Sin-Eater*.

The West Highland Railway links Fort William to Glasgow (August). The Highland Railway builds Britain's first 4–6–0 locomotives.

Strike by 65,000 coal miners from June to October. Twenty thousand steel workers laid off.

Sewage treatment system installed in Glasgow; raw sewage no longer flows into the Clyde.

Exhibition of Highland Industries in Inverness (September).

Edinburgh University awards medical degrees to women.

Severe hurricane causes damage across the south.

SFA Cup won by Rangers. Scotland beat England in Rugby International.

1895

Deer Commission schedules 1,782,785 acres of deer forest as suitable for crofting purposes.

Railway 'races to the north' cut London–Aberdeen journey to 8.5 hours.

Strike by 30,000 jute workers in Dundee.

Thirteen die in colliery explosion at Denny.

Completion of Sule Skerry lighthouse, most remote in Britain.

Theatre Royal, Glasgow, largest in the country, burns down, without casualties (March).

Exceptional snowfall in February.

SFA Cup won by Renton. Scotland beat England in Rugby International.

1896

James Connolly (1868–1916) leaves for Ireland.

1897

Charles Rennie Mackintosh designs the new Glasgow School of Art (completed 1899).

Andrew Usher, brewer, announces his gift of £100,000 to build a hall in Edinburgh.

First commercial cinematographic show, at the Empire in Edinburgh (April).

Alfred Austin, poet laureate, unveils the Burns statue in Irvine (18 July).

New Royal Observatory opens on Blackford Hill, Edinburgh.

Glasgow District Subway (electric) opens (14 December).

First large hydroelectric generating station, at Foyers.

Socialist Sunday schools begin in Glasgow (3 February).

SFA Cup won by Hearts. Scotland beat England in Rugby International.

1897

Formation of the Scottish Trades Union Congress (25 March). Establishment of the Congested Districts Board.

Sir Ronald Ross (1857–1932) identifies cause of malaria.

Dingwall–Skye Railway extended from Strome Ferry to Kyle of Lochalsh (November).

John Stirling makes first car to be assembled in Scotland: the Stirling.

Beacon fires from Caithness to the border mark Queen Victoria's Diamond Jubilee, and loyal demonstrations are held throughout the country (June).

SFA Cup won by Glasgow Rangers. England win Rugby International.

1898

Opening of the People's Palace, Glasgow (22 January).

Deer forests take up 2,510,625 acres.

Scottish Records Society founded.

Wireless telegraph in use.

Black houses are still being built on Lewis.

SFA Cup won by Rangers. Rugby International drawn with England.

1899

Boer War begins: Scottish regiments sent out to South Africa. Yeomanry units are mobilized, and troops' comforts' funds are started.

Assembly of Arrol-Johnson motor cars begins in Paisley.

Albion Motor Company established to build lorries (30 December).

SFA Cup won by Celtic. Scotland beat England in Rugby International.

1900

Dr Clark, the 'pro-Boer' Member of Parliament for Caithness, is burned in effigy in Thurso.

J P Coats of Paisley gives a library of books to each Board School, on condition they contain 'no religious works'.

Clyde shipbuilding totals 491,832 tons.

Scotland is now one of the world's main locomotive builders; more are built here than in England.

A Conciliation Board is established to fix miners' wages.

Free Church resolves on union with the United Presbyterian Church. Dissenters stay on and claim the Free Church's assets.

Unaccountable disappearance of the three Flannan Isles lighthouse keepers.

Smallpox in Glasgow results in 200 deaths.

Scotland has 65 poorhouses, capable of holding 15,500 people.

Argyll Motor Company opens (January).

Henhouses come into use.

Andrew Lang (1844–1912) publishes *History of Scotland*.

Gales cause damage to the Shetland fishing fleet (December).

SFA Cup won by Celtic. Rugby International drawn with England.

1901

Death of Queen Victoria. Accession of Edward I (VII of England).

Number of Gaelic speakers is 230,806; Gaelic-only speakers number 28,107.

Education Act makes 14 the school-leaving age; attendance at school compulsory for under-12s; exemptions are still possible for children aged 12–14.

Scottish Prohibition Party founded to promote abstention from alcohol.

George Douglas Brown (1869–1902) publishes *The House with the Green Shutters*.

Around this time, motor cars become increasingly frequent.

West Highland Railway extended to Mallaig (April).

On the Clyde, 519,000 tons of shipping are launched.

Andrew Carnegie offers £2,000,000 as a Trust Fund to the Scottish Universities. First Chair of Scottish History established, Edinburgh University.

Heavy gales in November disrupt the telegraphic link with England, and the coastguard vessel *Active* is wrecked on Granton breakwater, with 19 deaths.

SFA Cup won by Hibernian. Scotland beat England in Rugby International.

1902

Liberal League formed by Lord Rosebery for a 'sane imperialism', making a split with his leader, Campbell-Bannerman. Young Scots group formed to maintain the Gladstone tradition.

In Glasgow, a Citizens' Union is formed to protest at plans to build council houses.

Centenary number of the *Edinburgh Review* is published (October).

Hugh Miller's centenary is celebrated in Cromarty (August).

Sir Ronald Ross (1857–1932) wins the Nobel Prize for Medicine.

The United Free Church proceeds against Dr George Adam Smith, of its Theological College, for heresy: he is let off with a caution.

Glasgow's Hampden Park opened, world's largest stadium at the time.

In a whale hunt at Hillswick in Shetland, 166 whales are driven ashore and killed.

SFA Cup won by Rangers. England win Rugby International.

1903

Most industries depressed, especially steel and textiles. Shipbuilding on the Clyde is 484,853 tons. Wages reduced in the engineering, coal and steel industries. A strike of engineers is repudiated by the Amalgamated Society of Engineers.

North British Locomotive Company formed in Glasgow by amalgamation: largest privately owned locomotive works in Europe.

A train hits the buffers at St Enoch Station, Glasgow, causing 15 deaths (27 July).

Fire at Dailuaine (September 27) leads to 700,000 gallons of whisky being lost.

Serious flooding in the Clyde Valley causes extensive damage (February).

SFA Cup won by Celtic. Scotland beat England in Rugby International.

1904

Scottish Historical Review founded.

Scottish Motor Traction Company (SMT) founded (June), with first route from The Mound to Corstorphine.

Clyde shipbuilding is 417,876 tons. Sir William Ramsay (1851–1939), joint discoverer of argon, receives Nobel Prize for Chemistry.

The vessel *Scotia*, with the Scottish Antarctic Expedition, arrives in the Clyde (21 July).

Charles Rennie Mackintosh builds The Hill House, Helensburgh.

J M Barrie writes *Peter Pan*.

St Kildan wren protected by an Act of Parliament.

1905

SFA Cup won by Third Lanark. Scotland beat England in Rugby International.

1905

Royal Commission sits on the Scottish Ecclesiastical Question.

Edward VII reviews 38,000 Volunteers in Holyrood Park and a column of 10 motors.

Tonnage of ships launched on the Clyde amounts to 540,080. Beardmores take over Arrol-Johnson.

Gaelic admitted as an examination subject in schools.

Total eclipse of the sun visible in the south (30 September).

SFA Cup won by Third Lanark. Scotland beat England in Rugby International, but in their first International with New Zealand, Scotland lose 12–7, in Glasgow.

1906

Scottish Women's Suffragette Federation founded.

Shipbuilding tonnage is 601,658 tons. *Lusitania*, liner of 35,200 tons, is launched on the Clyde (7 June).

Strike by boilermakers and riveters for a five per cent pay rise (October–November) is defeated.

British Linen Company changes name to British Linen Bank.

Vatersay is 'invaded' by crofters from Barra, seeking more land.

New buildings of Marischal College, Aberdeen, opened (September) in time for University's 400th anniversary celebration.

Founding of the Glasgow Orpheus Choir by Hugh Roberton.

Scottish Labour Party founded. Socialist weekly *Forward* founded by Tom Johnston (October).

Serious railway accident with many deaths at Elliot Junction, Arbroath (28 December).

Earthquake shock felt in Perthshire.

Aberdeen is cut off for four days by snow (December).

SFA Cup won by Hearts. Scotland beat England in Rugby International. In first Rugby International with South Africa, Scotland win by two tries to nil.

1907

Scottish Grand Committee formed in Parliament.

Third Pan-Celtic Congress is held in Edinburgh.

Volunteer units are re-formed into the Territorial Army.

Clyde shipbuilding totals 619,919 tons.

Explosion at Ardeer nitroglycerine works kills three.

Caledonian Bank is merged into Bank of Scotland.

Failure of the Argyll Motor Company.

Universities of Edinburgh and Glasgow adopt the three-term system (previously two).

Campaign to preserve the Auld Brig of Ayr succeeds.

Movements are started for the cultivation, and increased use, of Scots and Gaelic.

Fifty small boats with holiday fishers are blown out to sea from Dunoon; most are recovered but two people drown (15 August).

Dr Bruce's Scottish Arctic Expedition, reported missing, turns up in north Norway.

SFA Cup won by Celtic. Scotland beat England in Rugby International.

1908

Scottish Liberal Federation supports disestablishment of the Church, votes for women and home rule (October).

School boards are required to ensure medical inspection of children and to provide meals in 'necessitous' cases.

Clyde shipbuilding falls to under 400,000 tons: lowest since 1894. Increasing unemployment creates disorder; workers try to force an entry into Glasgow City Hall. Trade and industry generally are depressed.

Interim report of Royal Commission on Whisky Industry declares that the name of whisky should not be denied to spirit made with malt, or with malt and grain.

The 10 Vatersay 'invaders' are each sentenced to 2 months in jail.

Royal Commission for the Inventory of Scottish Historical Monuments is established.

1909

Dunkeld Cathedral is restored.

Queen Victoria School, Dunblane, for the children of servicemen, is founded.

Fiftieth anniversary of the death of Robert Owen is commemorated in Lanark (6 June).

SFA Cup is won by Celtic. Scotland win Rugby International.

1909

Unemployment in the Glasgow area is estimated at 19 per cent of the work force.

Shipbuilding on the Clyde is 427,325 tons.

Campbeltown whisky output is down by 25 per cent.

Scottish Textiles College established at Galashiels.

Aberdeen imports 27,000 tons of Scandinavian granite for its granite-cutting and polishing industry.

Construction of a naval dockyard at Rosyth begins.

Legislation is made to preserve the Moray Firth fish stocks.

Glasgow Waterworks extended to Loch Arklet.

Marjorie Kennedy Fraser (1857–1930) publishes *Songs of the Hebrides*.

John Buchan (1875–1940) publishes *Prester John*.

Glasgow Repertory Theatre founded.

SFA Cup is withheld. Scotland beat England in Rugby International.

1910

Death of Edward VII. Accession of George V.

Twenty Liberal members set up a Scottish National Committee to promote self-government.

General Assembly of the Church of Scotland deplores the fall in the number of children attending Sunday schools.

First World Missionary Conference held in Edinburgh (14–23 June).

Iron ore deposits found on Raasay.

Death of William MacTaggart (born 1835), leading Scottish painter of his generation.

Production of knitted jerseys begins on Fair Isle.

James Braid (1870–1950) wins the Open Golf Championship for the fifth time. SFA Cup won by Dundee. England win Rugby International.

1911

Census shows the population as 4,760,904. Population of Glasgow now exceeds 1,000,000 (101,000 in 1811).

Scottish Unionist Party formed.

Coal Mines Act: boys under 13 no longer allowed to work underground.

Scottish Land Court set up.

Shipbuilding tonnage on the Clyde is 630,583.

Carters and dockers strike in Dundee; riots take place and the military are called in.

Quincentenary of St. Andrews University celebrated (13–15 September).

New Mitchell Library opened in Glasgow (16 October).

Chapel of the Thistle dedicated in St Giles, during a visit by King George V (19 July).

Heavy storms in December. Liner *Busiris* lost off the Galloway coast (23 December).

SFA Cup won by Celtic. England win Rugby International.

1912

Royal Commission on Housing set up (reported in 1917).

Scottish Board of Agriculture set up.

Crofters' Commission and Congested Districts' Board merged in Scottish Land Court.

Liberal Unionists merge with Conservative Unionists.

Young Scots group join with Liberal Home Rulers to promote self-government.

Coal strike in March involves 130,000 miners: additional 6d a day awarded.

Shipbuilding tonnage on the Clyde is 641,908 tons.

Textile industry benefits from economic recovery.

1913

Deer forests take up 3,584,966 acres.

Severe weather makes access to St Kilda impossible; HMS *Achilles* makes a relief visit.

SFA Cup won by Celtic. England win Rugby International.

1913

During the year, 36,000 people leave from the Clyde, mostly for Canada.

The number of Gaelic speakers is assessed at 202,398; Gaelic-only speakers number 18,400.

Government of Scotland bill (for home rule) dropped at the committee stage.

Temperance (Scotland) Act passed.

Scottish suffragettes begin sabotage operations, and burn church at Whitekirk.

Glasgow has 44,354 single-end houses; 111,451 room-and-kitchen houses, the vast majority sharing water closets.

Dockers of Leith strike from June to August; riots in July are met by naval and military force.

Shipbuilding tonnage is 756,976 tons. Liner *Aquitania* launched on the Clyde.

A record year for the jute industry.

SFA Cup won by Falkirk. England win Rugby International.

1914

War declared on Germany (August). Volunteers queque to join the army.

SFA Cup won by Celtic. England win Rugby International. Cup. International matches suspended until 1920.

1915

First wartime strikes on the Clyde: '2d an hour' strike of engineers (February); Rent Strike (October–November).

Major rail disaster at Quintinshill, Gretna, when troop train catches fire: 200 deaths.

HMS *Natal* blows up in the Cromarty Firth, with the loss of all hands (30 December).

Mary Slessor (born 1848), missionary, dies in Calabar, West
    Africa.

1916

HMS *Hampshire* sunk off Orkney; Lord Kitchener drowned.
Grand Fleet leaves Scapa Flow for Battle of Jutland (31 May).
Many Scottish troops killed in the Somme campaign.
Conscription to the armed forces is introduced.

1917

HMS *Vanguard* explodes in Scapa Flow: 804 killed.
Lord Leverhulme buys the island of Lewis (and Harris in 1919).
Sir J M Barrie publishes *Dear Brutus*. Norman Douglas
    publishes *South Wind*.

1918

First World War armistice (11 November).
Voting in Parliamentary elections extended to all men over 21
    and all women over 30.
Number of Scottish seats now 74.
Women can now stand for Parliament.
John Maclean, first Soviet consul, tried for sedition (May).
The *Iolaire*, with 200 returning soldiers and sailors, founders
    outside Stornoway Harbour (31 January): all are drowned.
School leaving age raised to 15 years. Catholic schools brought
    into the state education system.

1919

The German High Seas Fleet is scuttled in Scapa Flow (21
    June).
Riots in George Square, Glasgow, put down by tanks (31
    January). The 48-hour week is established for industry.
Shipbuilding tonnage is 2.6 million tons.
Housing and Town Planning (Scotland) Act.
Forestry Commission set up.
William Craigie proposes what will eventually become *The
    Scottish National Dictionary*.

1920

Massive slump in prices for agricultural produce.

Prohibition in the USA has a dire effect on whisky production and revenue.

Around this year the last cattle drove is made, from Knapdale to Stirling.

David Lindsay publishes *A Voyage to Arcturus*.

SFA Cup won by Kilmarnock. England win Rugby International.

1921

James Ramsay MacDonald forms first British Labour government.

Railways Act passed (19 August).

SFA Cup won by Partick Thistle. England win Rugby International.

1922

General election: Prohibitionist Party candidate defeats Winston Churchill in Dundee.

Return to Lanark from Canada of the silver badge from the box that held the Silver Bell, the world's oldest racing trophy.

First King's Cup Air Race, from Croydon to Glasgow and back (8–9 September).

SFA Cup won by Morton. England win Rugby International.

1923

First Scottish radio broadcasting station, in Glasgow.

Erection of Scottish National War Memorial by Sir Robert Lorimer (1864–1929), until 1928.

Disaster at Redding Colliery, Stirling: 40 miners killed.

Unemployment is at 14.3 per cent.

Highland, Caledonian and Glasgow and South-Western Railways are merged into the London, Midland and Scottish Railway (LMS); Great North of Scotland and North British are merged into the London and North-Eastern Railway (LNER).

Lord Leverhulme abandons efforts to modernize Lewis and Harris.

John MacLeod wins Nobel Prize for Medicine.

Royal Scottish Country Dance Society founded.

SFA Cup won by Third Lanark. England win Rugby International.

1924

George Buchanan's Home Rule Bill fails.

John Wheatley's Housing Bill is passed.

SFA Cup won by Airdrie. England win Rugby International.

1925

Sugar beet subsidy creates the sugar beet industry, until the 1970s.

SFA Cup won by Celtic. Scotland win Rugby International.

1926

Seven-month miners' strike leads to the General Strike (4–12 May).

Hugh MacDiarmid (1892–1978) publishes *A Drunk Man Looks at the Thistle*.

John Logie Baird (1888–1946) first demonstrates television (27 January).

Dundee Courier (1801) and *Advertiser* (1816) amalgamate.

SFA Cup won by St Mirren. Scotland win Rugby International.

1927

Unemployment is at 10.6 per cent.

Death of James Scott Skinner, fiddler and composer, 'The Strathspey king' (born 1843).

Last Arrol-Johnson cars are built, in Dumfries.

SFA Cup won by Celtic. Scotland beat England in Rugby International.

1928

Women receive the vote on same terms as men.

1929

Sir Alexander Fleming (1881–1955) discovers penicillin.

First plane to visit Lewis is seaplane S1058.

The 'Wembley Wizards' beat England 5–1 at football. SFA Cup won by Rangers. England win Rugby International.

1929

Local Government Act defines three classes of burgh: 4 cities, 19 large burghs, 178 small burghs. Parish councils abolished. Responsibility for poor relief, education and public health transferred to county councils and large burghs.

Unemployment is at 12.1 per cent.

Hunger march of unemployed from Glasgow to London.

Fire at Glen Cinema, Paisley: 70 people die (31 December).

John Logie Baird develops television transmission.

Church of Scotland and United Free Church amalgamate.

Usable reserves of iron ore are virtually exhausted; only 25,000 tons mined against 3,000,000 tons a year in the 1870s.

Last trams run in Perth (19 January).

SFA Cup won by Kilmarnock. Scotland win Rugby International.

1930

Rationalisation of the shipbuilding industry. Work on RMS *Queen Mary* suspended until 1933.

Inhabitants of St Kilda evacuated: island group now unpopulated.

Scottish Pipe Band Association formed.

United Services Museum set up in Edinburgh Castle.

SFA Cup won by Rangers. Rugby International drawn with England.

1931

Cuts in the pay of Naval personnel, up to 25 per cent, provoke a mutiny in the Atlantic Fleet on a visit to the Cromarty Firth. Ships are sent back to their home ports.

National Trust for Scotland founded.

The Scottish Youth Hostels Association and the Clarsach Society are formed.

Excavations begin at Jarlshof site in Shetland.

Neil Gunn (1891–1974) publishes *Morning Tide*.

Hannah Institute for Dairy Research founded.

SFA Cup won by Celtic. Scotland beat England in Rugby International.

1932

Unemployment is at 27.7 per cent.

Interest in Home Rule increases, as a possible answer to economic problems.

Edinburgh University celebrates its 350th anniversary (October).

Lewis Grassic Gibbon publishes *Sunset Song*, first in *Scots Quair* trilogy.

The *Flying Scotsman* train runs non-stop from London to Edinburgh in 7 hours 27 minutes, a record timing.

First combine harvester at work in Scotland.

SFA Cup won by Rangers. England win Rugby International.

1933

Labour gain control of Glasgow City Council.

The end of Prohibition in the USA leads to re-expansion of the whisky industry.

Scottish Milk Marketing Board created.

The Byre Theatre opens in St Andrews.

SFA Cup won by Celtic. Scotland beat England in Rugby International.

1934

Unemployment is at 23.1 per cent.

Kurt Hahn founds Gordonstoun School.

First internal airmail service in Britain, Inverness–Kirkwall.

RMS *Queen Mary* (81,235 tons) launched at Govan (28 September).

SFA Cup won by Rangers. England win Rugby International.

1935

William Soutar publishes *Poems in Scots*. Edwin Muir publishes *Scottish Journey*.

Export demand for cured herrings is down by two-thirds from pre-war years, home demand by one-third. Fishermen's earnings for the seaon average less than £10.

SFA Cup won by Rangers. Scotland win Rugby International.

1936

Death of George V. Accession and abdication of Edward II (VIII of England). Accession of George VI.

Saltire Society established.

Unemployment is at 18.7 per cent.

An estimated one million people watch the new *Queen Mary* leave the Clyde (24 March).

The LMS Railway's new Pacific locomotive runs from London to Glasgow in 5 hours 35 minutes.

SFA Cup won by Rangers. England win Rugby International.

1937

Building of St Andrew's House on Calton Hill, Edinburgh.

Scottish Gaelic Text Society established.

Scottish Special Housing Association established.

Trains collide at Castlecary (10 December): 35 dead, 179 injured.

World's largest football crowd recorded at Hampden Park for Scotland v England: 149,547.

SFA Cup won by Celtic. England win Rugby International.

1938

Unemployment is at 16.3 per cent and 22.8 per cent of Scottish working-class housing is classified as overcrowded.

The Iona Community is founded by Dr George MacLeod.

SFA Cup won by East Fife. Scotland beat England in Rugby International.

1939

Second World War begins. Conscription introduced.

Tom Johnston appointed Commissioner for Civil Defence.

Unemployment is at 13.5 per cent.

HMS *Royal Oak* sunk in Scapa Flow by a U-boat (14 October). First air raid of the war is aimed at Rosyth Naval Dockyard (16 October), and first German pilot of the war shot down over the Forth Bridge (16 October).

Disaster at Valleyfield Colliery, Fife: 35 miners killed.

SFA Cup won by Clyde. England win Rugby International. SFA Cup and Rugby International suspended until 1947.

1940

Evacuation of Dunkirk (1–4 June). Many Scots captured as Highland Division holds rearguard.

Formation of Local Defence Volunteers (later Home Guard).

Food rationing introduced.

Free milk provided to schools and to expectant mothers.

Marriage by declaration abolished.

RMS *Queen Elizabeth*, world's largest passenger steamer, launched on the Clyde (83,673 tons) and used first as a troopship.

1941

Tom Johnston appointed Secretary of State, February.

Bombing raids on Clydeside in spring, killing 1,200 people (March). Greenock raid in May leaves 280 dead.

Rudolf Hess, Hitler's deputy, lands in Scotland (10 May).

SS *Politician* wrecked (5 February): provides the story for Compton Mackenzie's *Whisky Galore*.

1942

Committee of Enquiry into Hydroelectricity recommends use of hydroelectric power to regenerate the Highlands (December).

Maximum penalty for black marketeering is raised to 14 years' penal servitude.

Personal petrol allowance abolished.

1943

Three-day gale in the north during January, with 100 mph winds; part of Peterhead Harbour is washed away.

1943

Hydroelectric Bill gets its second reading (24 February).

Bombing raid on Aberdeen leaves 43 dead.

Coal strikes intermittent between July and November.

Farm workers' pay is raised, to protests from farmers.

Glasgow Western Infirmary employs its first women doctors.

Glasgow Citizens' Theatre founded.

The remains of Pluscarden Priory presented to the Benedictine Order for restoration.

1944

HMS *Vanguard* launched on the Clyde (30 November): Britain's largest battleship at 44,500 tons.

Members of the Women's Land Army (4,400) are employed in Scotland. There is also a Women's Forestry Corps.

1945

Victory in Europe (8 May).

General election (5 July) with sweeping victory for Labour.

Sir Alexander Fleming is joint winner of the Nobel Prize for Medicine.

Choral Society formed at Haddo House, Edinburgh.

1946

Bread and flour rationing introduced (21 July).

Scottish National Party publishes its constitutional plan.

Scottish Games Association formed.

Strong winter gales, with 99 mph recorded at Stornoway.

1947

Coal mines brought into public ownership (1 January).

Scottish National Assembly takes place in Glasgow.

Unemployment is at 6 per cent.

Glasgow dockers' strike (March–May).

Coal exports resume, to Sweden and Ireland.

The *Caronia*, 34,000 tons, is launched on the Clyde (30 October).

Prestwick becomes a civil airport.

East Kilbride is Scotland's first 'New Town'.

A KLM plane crashes at Auchenweet Farm, Ayrshire: 39 killed.

Severest winter of the century.

First Edinburgh International Festival.

SFA Cup won by Aberdeen. England win Rugby International.

1948

National Health and National Insurance Acts passed (5 July). Much former social legislation, including the Poor Law Act, is repealed. Separate parliamentary seat for Scottish Universities is abolished.

Glenrothes becomes Scotland's second 'New Town'.

Miners moved from Lanark to Fife.

First performance since 1552 of Sir David Lindsay's *The Thrie Estaitis* at Edinburgh International Festival.

First post-war hydroelectric schemes at Loch Sloy, Loch Tummel and Fannich.

SFA Cup won by Rangers. Scotland beat England in Rugby International.

1949

John MacCormick (1904–61) organizes the Scottish Covenant for a Scottish Parliament within the UK; over a million sign.

Nobel Peace Prize is awarded to John Boyd Orr (1880–1971).

First 'forestry village' at Ae, Dumfriesshire.

Thirty thousand buyers come to Scottish Industries Exhibition in Glasgow.

Scottish Craft Centre established.

SFA Cup won by Rangers. England win Rugby International.

1950

General election: 37 Labour, 31 Tory, 2 Liberal, 1 Independent members returned.

Unemployment is at 2.7 per cent, twice the average for Great
Britain.

Tonnage of ships built on the Clyde is 444,000 tons.

Clydesdale and North of Scotland Banks merge.

Unauthorized removal of Stone of Scone (Stone of Destiny)
from Westminster.

Scottish National Orchestra founded.

St Salvator's College, St Andrews, celebrates its
quincentenary (27 August).

Sir Harry Lauder (born 1870), the archetypal Scots comedian,
dies on 26 February.

Scottish Mountain Rescue Committee formed.

SFA Cup won by Rangers. Scotland beat England in Rugby
International.

1951

General election: 35 Labour, 35 Conservative, 1 Liberal
members returned.

Census shows population of Scotland at 5,095,969, with
Glasgow 1,089,555 and Edinburgh 446,761.

Unemployment level is 2 per cent.

Coal production is at 23,526,000 tons.

Tonnage of ships built on the Clyde is 427,000 tons.

Total number of cattle is 1,600,000; of sheep 6,859,000; of
poultry 9,921,000. Working horses number 67,500. White
Fish Authority established.

Glasgow begins construction of 'high-rise' municipal flats.

The first National Nature Reserve is established, around
Beinn Eighe in Torridon. Pitlochry Festival Theatre is
established.

SFA Cup won by Celtic. England win Rugby International.

1952

Death of George VI. Accession of Elizabeth I (II of England)
with controversy over her title in Scotland.

Government sets up Royal Commission on Scottish Affairs.

Stone of Destiny turns up in Arbroath Abbey.

Whisky revenue to the Exchequer exceeds £60,000,000.

Bank of Scotland and the Union Bank amalgamate.

Television broadcasting begins from Kirk o' Shotts (4 March).

Twenty-seven thousand acres of new trees planted.

Highly successful herring season, 60 per cent up on 1951.

Foot and mouth disease, imported from the Continent, breaks out in Aberdeenshire (April–August): 19,000 animals are slaughtered.

Ospreys return to breed in the Cairngorms.

Outbreaks of myxomatosis kill off much of the rabbit population.

SFA Cup won by Motherwell. England win Rugby International.

1953

Food rationing abolished.

The *Prestwick Pioneer* is first plane to be designed and built in Scotland.

An experimental peat-burning power station is set up at Altnabreac, Caithness.

Royal yacht *Britannia* is launched on the Clyde.

Historic Buildings Council for Scotland established. Scottish Official Board of Highland Dancing established.

Whisky is recorded as Britain's biggest single export, by value. More record herring catches create a glut.

Great storm in January sinks passenger ferry *Princess Victoria* in North Channel (133 die); 47 million cubic feet of timber laid low by the gale.

SFA Cup won by Rangers. England win Rugby International.

1954

Crofters' Commission re-established.

Report of Royal Commission of 1951 makes no positive recommendations on devolution.

Tonnage of ships built on the Clyde is 477,805 tons.

1955

New brickworks established at Brora to use local clay.

Cairngorm National Nature Reserve established (9 July).

Fair Isle acquired by National Trust (4 September).

Uruguay beat Scotland 7–0 in football World Cup. SFA Cup won by Celtic. England win Rugby International.

1955

General election: 36 Conservative, 34 Labour, 1 Liberal returned. Scottish Standing Committee formed by Parliament.

Tonnage of ships built on the Clyde is 485,438 tons, highest since 1930.

Forth Road Tunnel mooted.

Beef cattle number 927,000; dairy cattle 797,000; sheep 7,336,000.

Heavy snow early in year isolates many communities.

Billy Graham, evangelist, claims 2.5 million people have heard his message (March–April).

SFA Cup won by Clyde. England win Rugby International.

1956

Cumbernauld 'New Town' started.

Five new coal pits sunk.

Chapelcross and Dounreay nuclear reactors begun.

Tonnage of coal mined in Scotland is 21,480,325 tons. Tonnage of steel produced is 2,518,900 tons. Tonnage of pig iron produced is 931,400 tons.

Scotland's 21st industrial estate is opened at Inverness (May).

Tramcars cease to run in Dundee (20 October) and Edinburgh (16 November). Electrification of Glasgow's suburban railways announced.

Unemployment is at 2.5 per cent.

National Library building opened (4 July).

Scottish Georgian Society established.

SFA Cup won by Hearts. England beat Scotland in Rugby International.

1957

Commercial television established.

Creation of the Ravenscraig Steelworks. Hunterston nuclear power station begun. Whiteinch Tunnel begun under the Clyde.

Abolition of horse-breeding grant spells the final end of the farm horse.

Sir Alexander Todd wins Nobel Prize for Chemistry.

Skiffle music is highly popular. Lonnie Donegan reaches No 1 in the hit parade with *Cumberland Gap*.

Rum, St Kilda and Caerlaverock are named as National Nature Reserves.

SFA Cup won by Falkirk. England win Rugby International.

1958

Unemployment at 4.4 per cent remains at double the average for Great Britain. Coal production falls below 20,000,000 tons, and the closure of 20 pits is forecast. Dixon's Blazes, the Govan ironworks, close after 119 years.

Last tram runs in Aberdeen.

Amalgamation of Scottish regiments is proposed, with controversy over whether combined Royal Scots Fusiliers and Highland Light Infantry (Royal Highland Fusiliers) should wear trews or kilt.

Hoard of 7th/8th-century silver found on St Ninian's Isle, Orkney.

SFA Cup won by Clyde. Rugby International drawn with England.

1959

General election: Labour majority in Scotland (38 Labour, 32 Conservative, 1 Liberal) but Conservatives win overall in Great Britain.

Oil and gas reserves discovered in the North Sea.

Auchengeich Colliery fire: 47 miners die.

The Broughty Ferry Lifeboat capsizes, with the loss of her crew (8 December).

1960

Unemployment is 4.3 per cent.

Deep-water terminal at Finnart constructed.

Industrial projects include steel-strip mill for Ravenscraig and wood-pulp mill for Corpach in Lochaber.

Tonnage of ships built on the Clyde is 388,539 tons.

Prestonpans Salt Works closes down.

National and Commercial Banks combine in National Commercial Bank.

Bovine tuberculosis finally eradicated. Cattle numbers total 1,892,411. Sheep population is highest ever at 8,883,659. The Deer Act is passed to conserve red deer stocks and prevent large-scale poaching.

The Church of Scotland rejects the 'Bishops' Report' (6 May). Iona Abbey, rebuilt, is reconsecrated (28 June).

SFA Cup won by St Mirren. Rugby International drawn with England.

1960

Announcement (November) of American nuclear submarine base in Holy Loch.

Employment Act encourages job creation.

National service is abolished.

Lothian shale mining comes to an end. Shipbuilding orders fall.

Cattle numbers exceed 2,000,000 for first time. Working horses are now down to 18,294.

North Ford Causeway joins Benbecula to South Uist. Queen Elizabeth makes the first visit to Shetland by its reigning monarch since Haakon IV in 1263.

Six towns begin to bid for a new university.

Oxford and Cambridge expedition to Loch Ness reports inconclusive findings.

SFA Cup won by Rangers. England win Rugby International.

1961

Census records population at 5,178,490. Number of Gaelic-speakers 76,580; number of Gaelic-only speakers 1,097.

Plebiscite Fund opened to seek £100,000 to ascertain people's view on self-government (31 November).

Demonstrations take place against Holy Loch Polaris base, as USS *Proteus* arrives to set up depot on 3 March.

Seaforth and Cameron Highlanders combined in a single regiment as Queen's Own Highlanders.

Muriel Spark (1918–) publishes *The Prime of Miss Jean Brodie*.

Toothill Report on Scottish economy (22 November) asks for more industrial/commercial planning by government.

Rocket-firing range set up on South Uist.

Lorries being assembled at Bathgate by BMC, and Rootes Group announce car factory for Linwood.

Ben Cruachan pumped storage hydroelectric scheme and Greenock Dry Dock begun.

Scottish fishing industry numbers 3,000 vessels. Aberdeen trawler *Red Crusader* is shelled by a Danish warship off the Faeroes.

SFA Cup won by Dunfermline. England win Rugby International.

1962

King Olaf of Norway makes state visit to Edinburgh.

Moderator of the Church of Scotland makes historic visit to the Pope.

Establishment of Livingston 'New Town'.

Unemployment is at 4.7 per cent. Sixteen further collieries are closed down, and 27 listed for closure.

Glasgow tramways close down (4 September), with last tram to Auchenshuggle.

Wood-pulp mill established at Corpach.

Foundation of Scottish Opera (28 January).

Fixed Sunday opening hours for pubs spell the end of the 'bona-fide traveller' era. Glasgow opens the first municipal anti-smoking clinic.

1963

SFA Cup won by Rangers. Rugby International drawn with England.

1963

The Reid Committee proposes sweeping changes in land law, first since 1617.

Scottish peers are all made eligible to sit in House of Lords: previously they elected 16 of their number.

Last capital punishment in Scotland: Henry Burnett is hanged for murder at Craiginches Jail, Aberdeen.

The Beeching Report heralds sweeping cuts in railway services.

Rootes car factory opens at Linwood (2 May), making Hillman Imp car. Denny's Shipyard on the Clyde goes into liquidation; Harland & Wolff at Govan is put on a care-and-maintenance basis. Work begins on Tay Road Bridge (29 March).

The Royal College of Science and Technology, Glasgow, becomes University of Strathclyde.

Aberdeen trawler *Millwood* is arrested by Icelandic gunboat *Odinn* (28 April).

SFA Cup won by Rangers. England win Rugby International.

1964

General election (October): Labour government at Westminster. Scottish result: Labour 42, Conservative 26, Liberal 4.

Harris tweed established by law as a product spun and finished in the Outer Hebrides.

Scotland's railway network substantially reduced, including many branch lines and Stranraer–Dumfries main line.

Forth Road Bridge opened (4 September), also first stretch of M8 motorway (20 November).

Contract signed for construction of *Queen Elizabeth II* at Clydebank.

Proposal for Solway Barrage Scheme published (August).

Typhoid outbreak in Aberdeen leads to 400 cases of typhoid, from corned beef (May–June).

Stirling selected as site for a new university (17 July). Queen's College, Dundee, gains university status (16 September).

The Kirk refuses to have women ministers.

SFA Cup won by Rangers. Scotland beat England in Rugby International.

1965

Establishment of the Scottish Law Commission and the Highlands and Islands Development Board.

Capital punishment abolished.

Post Office Savings Bank HQ to be moved to Glasgow. Cruachan Hydroelectric Scheme opens (15 October).

First Sunday ferry to Skye meets a hostile demonstration.

Ingliston racing circuit opened (11 April).

Princes Street Station, Edinburgh, closes (September).

Heriot-Watt College, Edinburgh, becomes a university.

SFA Cup won by Celtic. Rugby International drawn with England.

1966

General election: Labour government returned at Westminster. Scottish result: Labour 46, Conservative 24, Liberal 3.

Royal Commission on Scottish Local Government is set up.

Unemployment is at 3.6 per cent.

Geddes Report calls for reorganisation of shipbuilding into larger units.

Redundancies begin at Bathgate and Linwood motor plants; workers reject work-sharing.

Major gas discoveries in the North Sea.

Tay Road Bridge opened (18 August).

Two Glasgow railway stations, St Enoch and Buchanan Street, close down.

General Assembly of the Kirk allows women elders.

General Teaching Council for Scotland set up.

1967

Historical Dictionary of Scottish Gaelic begun.

Smallest public theatre in the world is opened at Dervaig, Mull.

SFA Cup won by Rangers. Scotland beat England in Rugby International. Walter McGowan wins the World Flyweight title (14 June).

1967

Scottish National Party wins Hamilton by-election.

Establishment of the Scottish Arts Council and Scottish Civic Trust.

Unemployment is at 3.8 per cent.

Clyde shipbuilding rationalized into two consortia. *Queen Elizabeth II* launched at Clydebank (20 September).

Last steam puffer in general trade, the *Invercloy*, is broken up.

Fire at Michael Colliery, East Wemyss: 9 men are killed, and the pit is closed down.

Biggest ever pearl found in the Tay, at 44.5 grams; christened 'Wee Willie'.

SFA Cup won by Celtic, who are also the first British side to win the European Cup, in Lisbon. England win Rugby International.

1968

Countryside Commission for Scotland established.

Scottish Transport Group set up to co-ordinate steamer and bus schedules.

The Cameronians regiment is disbanded. Argyll and Sutherland Highlanders also to be disbanded.

Irvine 'New Town' founded.

Decimal coinage is introduced (23 April).

Hurricane force gales cause 20 deaths (15 January).

Glasgow warehouse fire leads to the death of 22 people (18 November).

The Church of Scotland allows women to become licensed as ministers.

SFA Cup won by Dunfermline. England win Rugby International. Jim Clark, three times world motor racing champion, killed in a crash at Hockenheim, Germany (7 April). Andrew Cowan and Brian Coyle win London–Sydney Car Rally (18 December).

1969

Age of majority and voting lowered to 18 years. Scottish Select Committee set up in Parliament.

Wheatley Report on Local Government. Three Glasgow Labour councillors jailed for corruption: London HQ takes over the Glasgow Labour Party.

British Linen Bank merges with Bank of Scotland.

The Waverley rail route from Edinburgh via Hawick to Carlisle closes (5 January). The Edinburgh–Perth route closes (15 October).

Burntisland Shipbuilding Company goes bankrupt.

Aberdeen trawlermen strike (June–August).

Scottish Fisheries Museum set up at Anstruther.

Mgr Gordon Gray becomes Scotland's first resident cardinal since before the Reformation (April).

The Longhope Lifeboat founders in the Pentland Firth, with the loss of her crew of eight (18 March).

A gunman is shot dead in Glasgow after wounding 12 people.

SFA Cup won by Celtic. England win Rugby International.

1970

General election: 44 Labour, 23 Conservative, 3 Liberal, 1 Nationalist members. Scottish Labour majority outweighed by Tory win in England. Conservative government formed.

Argyll and Sutherland Highlanders are 'reprieved', though only at Company strength.

Unemployment at 103,000 is highest for eight years.

Hydroelectric power schemes now number 54.

Home (UK) sales of whisky exceed 10,000,000 gallons for the first time. Export sales are 62,000,000 gallons.

Albion Motor Company becomes part of British Leyland.

Open University founded, with Scottish network.

M8 motorway completed from Edinburgh to Glasgow.

Fraserburgh Lifeboat founders; only one of her crew survives (21 January).

SFA Cup won by Aberdeen. Scotland win Rugby International.

1971

Census records population as 5,230,000.

British Summer Time is ended: mornings are lighter.

Argyll and Sutherland Highlanders are restored to battalion strength. Royal Scots Greys and Third Carabiniers are combined in Royal Scots Dragoon Guards (2 July).

Crisis, work-in and demonstrations at Upper Clyde Shipbuilders.

Scottish fishing industry numbers 2,600 vessels.

Invergordon Aluminium Works begin production (25 May).

Collapse of safety barriers in Ibrox Stadium causes 66 deaths. Gas explosion at Clarkston kills 21 (21 October).

Government ceases distribution of free milk to schools.

A bomb explodes at Edinburgh Castle during the Military Tattoo (28 August).

SFA Cup won by Celtic. Centennial Rugby International, Scotland beat England. Chay Blyth sails single-handed 'wrong way' around the world. Ken Buchanan wins World Lightweight Boxing Championship (12 February).

1972

Britain joins the European Common Market (22 January).

A new 'cod war' with Iceland begins.

Rockall formally annexed by the United Kingdom as part of Scotland (11 February).

Edinburgh has a Labour Lord Provost for the first time.

Local authorities clash with the government over imposing increases in council house rents. Court of Session instructs Glasgow to comply.

Students at Stirling University demonstrate against cost of the Queen's visit.

George Mackay Brown publishes *Greenvoe*.

Royal Scots Dragoon Guards reach No. 1 in the hit parade with their recording of *Amazing Grace*.

Unemployment is at 5.8 per cent in December. Workers at British Leyland, Bathgate, strike for 9 weeks (February–March).

Major North Sea oil activity includes digging of the world's largest graving dock, at Nigg.

Seven men are lost with the *Nautilus* of Fraserburgh (January).

Seven firefighters die in a fire in Glasgow (August).

SFA Cup won by Celtic. Scotland beat England in Rugby International. Rangers win European Cup in Barcelona, but fans' behaviour brings them a two-year suspension from European competition.

1973

Kilbrandon Report recommends some form of Scottish Assembly.

Clydebank is fined twice for not implementing council house rent rises.

Clayson Committee recommends changes in licensing hours.

Oil shortage results in the 'three-day week'.

Unemployment is at 3.7 per cent.

Piper and Thistle oil fields discovered. St Fergus gas terminal approved (September).

First strike of firefighters in Glasgow (26 October–4 November).

Work begins on Strathclyde Regional Park, at Hamilton.

The 7:84 Theatre Company produces John McGrath's *The Cheviot, the Stag, and the Black, Black Oil*.

Death on 5 December of Sir Robert Watson-Watt, inventor of radar (born 1892).

SFA Cup won by Celtic. England win Rugby International.

1974

Jackie Stewart, three times world champion racing driver, retires (October). Scotland through to finals of the 1974 World Cup.

1974

Two general elections, with Scottish results helping to secure minority Labour government and then a small majority for the same party; 11 Nationalist MPs elected (October). Scottish Council of Labour rejects its own executive's opposition to a Scottish Assembly. Scotland experiences net immigration for the first time since 1945: arrivals exceed departures by 7,800.

Ninian oil field discovery announced (2 April). Sullom Voe and Flotta oil terminal plans agreed. *Highland One*, world's largest oil platform, launched at Nigg (16 August). Petrol supplies restricted by tanker drivers' strike, (May–June).

Glasgow's *Evening Citizen* ceases publication.

Professional football played on Sunday for the first time (27 January).

SFA Cup won by Celtic. Scotland beat England in Rugby International. Scotland exit from World Cup.

1975

Referendum on membership of European Community: 1,332,286 in favour, 948,039 against; only Shetland and the Western Isles record a majority against it (6 June).

Reform of local government: new local authorities established: 9 regions, 53 districts and 3 island councils replace 430 previous councils.

Scottish Development Agency established.

Convention of Royal Burghs becomes Convention of Scottish Local Authorities. Scottish Ombudsman (Commissioner for Local Administration) appointed in August.

King Carl Gustav of Sweden makes a state visit (8–10 July).

Announcement of nuclear power station for Torness (February).

Govan Shipbuilders receive £17.2 million of state aid.

Headquarters of British National Oil Corporation to be in Glasgow.

'Tartan Army' claims responsibility for bomb damage to pipelines; six members of the Army of Provisional Government jailed (April and May).

Troops move 70,000 tons of Glasgow's rubbish during dustmen's strike.

The Bay City Rollers reach No 1 in the hit parade with *Bye Bye Baby*.

Dougal Haston and Doug Scott climb Everest by the southwest face for the first time (September).

Scottish Football League restructured: Premier Division has 10 clubs, First Division has 14, Second Division has 14. SFA Cup won by Celtic. England win Rugby International.

1976

Crofting Reform Act enables crofters to buy their land. Licensing (Scotland) Act passed. Divorce Act abolishes 'matrimonial offence' as cause and substitutes 'irretrievable breakdown of marriage'.

William Ross, longest-serving Secretary of State, resigns.

Two Scottish MPs form a breakaway Scottish Labour Party.

'Scotland is British' pro-union campaign launched on 23 November.

Unemployment 7.5 per cent.

Base of the world's largest concrete structure, for the Ninian field, is floated out of Loch Kishorn.

Canonisation of St John Ogilvie (17 October).

Exceptionally hot and dry summer this year.

SFA Cup won by Rangers. Scotland beat England in Rugby International.

1977

Scottish National Party make large gains in local elections.

Unemployment 8.4 per cent.

Boilermakers agree to end demarcation at Govan Shipbuilders.

1978

Flotta oil terminal inaugurated.

First licences are granted for Sunday opening of pubs (October).

Scottish football fans dig holes in the Wembley pitch, London, after 2–1 win over England in soccer international.

SFA Cup won by Celtic. England beat Scotland in Rugby International. Scotland through to the finals of the 1978 World Cup.

1978

Unemployment falls during the year from 9.2 per cent to 7.8 per cent.

British Leyland factory in Bathgate is on strike for seven weeks (August–September): the company announces reduced investment in the plant. Chrysler plant at Linwood on strike for five weeks (July–August). Singer factory at Dumbarton is largely shut down (December). Last open-hearth steel works, at Glengarnock, shuts down (December).

Herring fishing banned on west coast, except for the Firth of Clyde, to conserve stocks.

Protests lead to reduction of a planned large-scale seal cull in Orkney.

SFA Cup won by Rangers. England wins Rugby International. Scotland exits from the World Cup, winning one out of three games.

1979

Devolution Referendum fails to gain the necessary support of 40 per cent of the electorate: 1,230,937 in favour – 32.85 per cent; 1,153,503 against – 30.78 per cent; 36.37 per cent abstain (1 March).

General election returns Tories to Westminster under Mrs Thatcher (4 May). In Scotland, Labour have 44 seats, Tories 22, Liberals 3, SNP 2. First European elections arouse little interest (8 August).

Lorry drivers' strike paralyses much of industry and commerce in January. Scottish branch of Confederation of British Industry asks churches to pray for industrial peace. Collapse of Penmanshiel Tunnel disrupts east coast railway line from Edinburgh to Newcastle.

Iona is acquired by the Sir Hugh Fraser Trust.

Extremely cold weather enables first Grand Bonspiel for sixteen years to be played on Lake of Menteith (February).

SFA Cup won by Rangers. Rugby International drawn with England. Jim Watt wins World Lightweight Boxing title.

1980

Scottish Radio Orchestra is disbanded by the BBC, but Scottish Symphony Orchestra is retained.

Alan Wells wins the Olympic Gold Medal in the 100 Metres.

Earthquake, centred on Longtown, Cumbria, affects the south-west.

SFA Cup won by Celtic. England wins Rugby International.

1981

Unemployment at 325,000.

The Linwood car plant is closed down with loss of 4,500 jobs; Bathgate tractor plant and Corpach wood-pulp mill also close.

More than 40,000 people now work in the electronics industry, and around 100,000 in oil-related industries.

Alasdair Gray publishes *Lanark*.

Glasgow University opens a Science Park.

Death of Sir William MacTaggart (born 1903), central artist of the Edinburgh school and grandson of William MacTaggart.

SFA Cup won by Rangers. England win Rugby International.

1982

Unemployment at 333,000.

The Carron Iron Company goes into liquidation, and the aluminium works at Invergordon is closed down.

Work begins on Coulport nuclear submarine base.

1983

Pope John Paul II visits Scotland (May).

Most local authorities ban corporal punishment in schools after an adverse European Court decision.

SFA Cup won by Aberdeen. Rugby International drawn with England. Jocky Wilson is World Professional Darts Champion (again in 1989).

1983

General election: Labour have 41 seats, Tories 21, Liberal/SDP 8; Nationalists 2.

A new coal mine opens, at Castlebridge, near Kincardine.

Scott-Lithgow Yard has an £85,000,000 oil rig cancelled: 4,000 jobs lost.

Unemployment at 311,500.

Opening of the Burrell Collection galleries in Glasgow (October).

Following purification schemes, salmon are once again found in the River Clyde after more than 100 years.

SFA Cup won by Aberdeen, who also win European Cup-Winners' Cup. Scotland win Rugby International.

1984

Election for European Parliament: Tories lose 3 of their 4 seats; Labour now have 4, the SNP one.

Coal miners' strike.

The Burrell Collection is Scotland's biggest visitor attraction.

Unemployment is at 326,000 (December). Scotland has three of Great Britain's ten unemployment 'black spots'; one of them is Irvine.

North Sea oil production is 127 million tonnes – fifth most productive in the world.

SFA Cup won by Aberdeen. Scotland beats England in Rugby International and wins the Grand Slam.

1985

Unemployment at a postwar record, with 340,000 out of work.

Property revaluation causes large rises in rates.

Teachers on strike throughout the year for an independent pay review body, and many schools provide only part-time education.

Oil production is at record level.

The wettest summer on record. Hay production is down 85 per cent in some areas.

The High Court rejects the claim of two brothers to the right of trial by combat.

Ex-SAS man Tom McClean lives on Rockall for 40 days.

SFA Cup won by Celtic. England wins Rugby International. Scotland through to finals of the Football World Cup. Sandy Lyle wins te Golf Open.

1986

Edinburgh hosts the Commonwealth Games, but 31 countries boycott the event as a protest against sporting links with South Africa. Games have a £4,000,000 deficit.

Edinburgh has a fast-growing HIV/AIDS problem.

Riots and disturbances in several prisons, including Perth, Saughton, Peterhead and Barlinnie.

Falling oil prices cause recession in the oil industry and more widely. Gartcosh steel-rolling mill closes.

First drive-on car ferries to Lewis.

A Chinook helicopter crashes near Sumburgh Head, with the loss of 45 lives.

Fall-out effects from the Chernobyl nuclear disaster are found throughout the country, especially on uplands.

SFA Cup won by Aberdeen. Scotland win Rugby International. Scotland exits from the World Cup tournament.

1987

General election: Conservatives returned to power at Westminster but win only 10 out of 72 Scottish seats: their 'right to govern' is questioned. Mrs Thatcher, Prime Minister, dismisses prospect of devolution.

1988

After two and a half years of strikes, teachers win a pay increase but with stringent service conditions (January).

Disruption in prisons continues. Governors complain about conditions (3 March).

SFA Cup won by St Mirren. England wins Rugby International. Dundee United fails to win the UEFA Cup, but their fans win a good behaviour award.

1988

Privatization of the two electricity boards announced.

Fire on the Piper Alpha oil rig in the North Sea kills 166 men (6 July).

A terrorist bomb brings down a Pan-Am jumbo jet on Lockerbie, causing the deaths of 259 passengers and 11 inhabitants of the town.

James Whyte Black wins Nobel Prize for Medicine.

Glasgow hosts the Third International Garden Festival.

Seafield Colliery in Fife is closed.

SFA Cup won by Celtic. England wins Rugby International.

1989

Poll Tax is introduced in Scotland as a trial for UK. Protests increase throughout the year.

Government launches a Rural Enterprise Programme to help rural industry.

Two of the three remaining Scottish collieries are closed.

A nuclear re-processing plant is announced for Dounreay; environmentalists launch protest movement.

Torrential rain causes flood in Inverness and washes away the Ness railway viaduct.

SFA Cup is won by Celtic. England wins Rugby International. Richard Corsie is World Indoor Bowling Champion (again in 1991).

1990

Glasgow is European City of Culture.

Half a million people have not paid Poll Tax.

Sale of council homes to tenants reaches 200,000.

Electronic products form 42 per cent of manufactured exports. Scotland is estimated to produce a third of Europe's personal computers.

Clydesdale Tube Works, Bellshill, closes down (November).

Fishing vessel *Antares* sunk by a submarine in the Firth of Clyde; Royal Navy promises better information on submarine movements.

Gold-panning classes are given at Sanquhar.

Scotland exits from Football World Cup in first round. SFA Cup won by Celtic. Scotland wins Rugby's Grand Slam and Calcutta Cup in final match of the season, at Murrayfield. Stephen Hendry is World Snooker Champion (again in 1992).

1991

£1,000 million of Poll Tax estimated as unpaid, since its introduction. Poll Tax replaced by new Council Tax.

Farm incomes estimated as 27 per cent down on year before.

Western Isles Council loses investment of £24,000,000 with the collapsed BCCI bank.

Unemployment level 9.2 per cent in June.

Shipbuilding now employs 14,000 compared to 77,000 in 1951.

SFA Cup won by Motherwell. England wins Rugby International. Liz McColgan is World Champion in Women's 10,000 metres.

1992

General election returns 11 Tories (up 2) and only 3 SNP.

Unemployment is almost 250,000.

Scotland estimated as fourth largest financial centre in Europe: 220,000 people are employed in the financial sector (11 per cent of the work force).

4,000 fishermen and their families demonstrate against EU fishing quotas.

1993

United States' Polaris base at Holy Loch is closed down.

Centennial National Mod takes place in Oban.

Unemployment almost at 250,000 people. Four out of ten manufacturing jobs in Scotland are estimated to have disappeared since 1979. Ravenscraig Steelworks is closed down (June).

SFA Cup won by Rangers. England win Rugby International.

1993

Strong opposition is made to government plans to privatize Scottish water supplies.

Unemployment at 9.2 per cent (December).

£1,300 million plan to prolong activity in the Brent oilfield until 2008.

Ten of Scotland's fifteen largest companies are in the financial sector; 20 companies produce 60 per cent of exports: these are mostly to Europe.

Timex factory in Dundee closes after a long dispute between management and work force.

Oil tanker *Braer* runs aground off Shetland (5 January): 85,000 tonnes of oil are spilled but stormy weather prevents pollution disaster.

Irvine Welsh publishes *Trainspotting*.

SFA Cup won by Rangers. England win Rugby International.

1994

Scotland's 65 regional and district councils are replaced by 28 single-tier authorities.

Elections for European Parliament return 5 Labour and one Nationalist MEPs.

Scottish National Party holds its 60th Annual Conference, in Inverness.

John Smith MP, Leader of the Labour Party and MP for Monklands, dies.

Unemployment is at 8.7 per cent.

De-commissioning of the Dounreay atomic reactor announced.

Go-ahead is given for developing the first oilfields to the west of Shetland.

Edinburgh HQ of British Gas is closed down.

A Chinook helicopter crashes on the Mull of Kintyre, killing all on board. Official report blames pilot error.

James Kelman publishes *How Late It Was, How Late*, and wins the Booker Prize.

Severe flooding in the Paisley area after torrential rain (10–11 December).

Football League establishes a Third Division, making four in all. SFA Cup won by Dundee United. England win Rugby International.

1995

Scottish National Party wins Perth and Kinross by-election, pushing Tories into third place after Labour.

Unemployment at its lowest level in fifteen years.

Scottish nuclear plants to be privatized with English ones despite protests but HQ of new company to be in Edinburgh.

A Taiwanese company announces plans to develop the Ravenscraig Steelworks site for an electronics plant, with 3,000 jobs.

Assynt crofters in dispute with landowner.

Ten people die in climbing accidents between January and March.

The number of drug-related deaths in Strathclyde causes concern.

Opening of the Skye bridge over Kyle Akin, with controversial toll charges (16 October).

SFA Cup won by Celtic. England win Rugby International.

1996

The Stone of Destiny is ceremonially returned to Scotland and placed in Edinburgh Castle.

Fifteen Labour councillors in Monklands District are suspended from office.

1997

Unemployment is at 7.9 per cent.

Hyundai announce a large electronic project centred near Dunfermline.

Proposed University of the Highlands and Islands receives a Millennium Commission grant of £30,000,000.

Sixteen children and their teacher are killed by a gunman in their school in Dunblane (16 March).

In Lanarkshire and surrounding areas of Central Scotland, 15 people die and some 50 are hospitalized because of *E. coli* 0157 food poisoning. About 400 people are affected (November–December) and 5 more people have died by June 1997.

The Rosyth Naval Dockyard sold to a private company (November).

A girl first bears the standard at Duns Common Riding.

SFA Cup won by Rangers. England win Rugby International.

1997

Government announces the establishment of an independent Food Safety Council (January).

Chairman of the Scottish Conservative Party, Sir Michael Hirst, resigns (March).

General election (1 May): no Conservative MPs are returned in Scotland. Labour government formed.

Devolution Referendum results in vote for a Scottish Parliament with tax-varying powers.

Following public pressure over the Dunblane shootings, MPs vote to make the ownership of all handguns illegal from autumn 1997 (June).

A report is made on the *E coli* 0157 outbreak by Professor Hugh Pennington with 32 recommendations for improving hygiene in shops, abattoirs and farms.

The island of Eigg is bought by its inhabitants for £1.5 million.

Scientists at Roslin Institute breed a sheep by cloning. She is named 'Dolly' (February).

Four fishermen drown when their boat capsizes 100 miles off the Scottish coast.

Serious flooding occurs in northern Scotland as more than three inches of rain falls in 36 hours (2 July).

SFA cup won by Kilmarnock. England win Rugby International with their highest score in a home international.

1998

Government announces that the Dounreay nuclear plant is to close. Gus MacDonald, chairman of Scottish Media Group, made a life peer and Minister at the Scottish Office.

Dr Ian Oliver, Chief Constable of Grampian, forced to resign by Donald Dewar, Scottish Secretary.

Silvery Sea, Scottish trawler, struck by a German coaster: five fishermen drown.

Four climbers die after being hit by an avalanche on Ben Nevis; three others survive.

Museum of Scotland opened by Queen Elizabeth in Edinburgh.

John Barr, the butcher whose contaminated meat caused the *E coli* outbreak in Lanarkshire, is fined £2,250.

Stephen Hendry defeated in Snooker World Championships: first time since 1990. SFA cup won by Hearts. Scotland knocked out of the World Cup in the first round. Rugby International won by England.

1999

Elections for the first Scottish Parliament (May) return 62 Labour, 38 SNP, 22 Conservative, 18 Liberal-Democrat, 1 Green, 1 Scottish Socialist and 1 Independent MSPs.

Queen Elizabeth opens Scottish Parliament (1 July). Donald Dewar is First Minister; David Steel is President.

Glasgow is UK City of Architecture and Design this year.

A Cessna plane crashes near Glasgow Airport: eight die and three survive (September).

Last solar eclipse of the millennium is seen in partial form across Scotland.

2000

The Sutherland Royal Commission on care for the old recommends universal free care for old age pensioners (March).

The Kingston Bridge in Glasgow is moved two inches by hydraulic jacks.

A Larkhall family are killed in a gas explosion that totally destroys their home.

British Open Golf Championship at Carnoustie is won by Paul Lawrie from Stonehaven. SFA cup won by Rangers. Euro 2000 play-offs: Scotland beat England 1–0 at Wembley; England beat Scotland 2–0 at Hampden Park. Craig Brown, Scotland manager receives the CBE. Scotland are Five Nations Rugby Champions.

2000

Flu outbreak is the worst in 10 years. Hospitals under pressure.

The *Solway Harvester* fishing boat sinks off the coast of the Isle of Man: all 7 crew are lost.

Scottish Parliament agrees that Scottish students who study at Scottish Universities will have their tuition fees paid by the state.

Two Libyans are accused of the bombing of the Pan-Am Flight 103 which crashed over Lockerbie in 1988. Scots Law trial begins in Holland (May).

Sean Connery receives a knighthood.

Scottish Qualifications Authority chief, Ron Tuck, resigns after 5,000 pupils receive the wrong Higher and Standard Grade exam results or do not receive any at all.

Three days of blockades of fuel depots by truckers, haulage firms and farmers in protest against the level of Fuel Tax. Petrol shortage lasts for over a week.

Donald Dewar, First Minister, has an operation in May to replace a faulty heart valve; he returns to work three months later but dies following a brain haemorrhage on 11 October.

Henry MacLeish is elected First Minister. John Swinney is elected leader of the Scottish National Party following Alex Salmond's resignation.

Michael Martin MP is elected Speaker of the House of Commons, first Catholic to hold this post since the Reformation.

British Open Golf Championship is held at St Andrews: won by Tiger Woods of the USA. Celtic is knocked out of the SFA cup by Inverness Caledonian Thistle. Rangers win the League Championship and the SFA Cup. England wins the Six Nations Rugby Championship; Scotland win the Calcutta Cup. David Coulthard wins Monaco Grand Prix.

2001

Election for Westminster Parliament (June): Labour win 56 seats, Liberal Democrats 9, SNP 5, Conservatives 1.

Scottish Parliament agrees to advance proposals for universal free care of old age pensioners (25 January).

House of Lords votes to set up a select committee to reinvestigate the Mull of Kintyre Chinook crash of 1994.

The extra-territorial court at Camp Zeist, Netherlands, finds Abdel Baset Al-Megrahi guilty of the murder of 270 people at Lockerbie, and sentences him to life imprisonment. The second accused Libyan is acquitted. The trial is estimated to have cost £62,000,000.

Severe outbreak of foot-and-mouth disease from England affects many farms in Dumfries and Galloway, with many thousands of animals slaughtered and burned.

Cardinal Thomas Winning dies (June).

Plans to spread asylum seekers throughout the UK include 3,700 additional places in Glasgow.

New plans for the derelict Ravenscraig Steelworks site in Motherwell as a recreation and retail complex.

Scottish Parliament votes for a ban on foxhunting and other hunting with dogs.

Henry MacLeish resigns as First Minister (October) and Jack McConnell is elected as Scotland's third First Minister (November).

Scottish tourism industry hit hard by the after-effects of the foot-and-mouth outbreak and the terrorist attacks on the Pentagon and twin towers of New York's World Trade Centre on 11 September.

John Higgins completes a hat-trick in snooker: the Champions Cup, Regal Masters and Stan James British Open. Stephen Hendry wins the European Open. Celtic win 'The Treble': Scottish Championship, SFA Cup and the CIS Insurance Cup. England win the Six Nations Rugby Championship and the Calcutta Cup.

Index